Portland Potpourri:
ART, FOUNTAINS
& OLD FRIENDS

WEST SLOPE COMMUNITY LIBRARY
3678 SW 78th
MEMBER OF
WASHINGTON COUNTY COOPERATIVE
LIBRARY SERVICES

BY THE SAME AUTHOR

Early Portland: Stump-Town Triumphant
Rival townsites on the Willamette
River, 1831-1854, and Portland's
victory in the battle to become
Oregon's metropolis.

Portland Names and Neighborhoods: Their Historic Origins
More than 950 street, school, and
park names of Portland, Oregon,
with biographical and historical
information about their origins.

Skidmore's Portland: His Fountain and Its Sculptor
Victorian Portland, from the 1850s
to the 1880s, as seen through the
life of Stephen Skidmore. Includes
a biography of Olin Warner, the
sculptor of Portland's famous
Skidmore Fountain.

We Claimed This Land: Portland's Pioneer Settlers
Biographies of the 212 pioneers who
first owned the land that is now
Portland, Oregon. Many of these
first settlers acquired their land free
under the Donation Land Act.

Portland Potpourri:
ART, FOUNTAINS & OLD FRIENDS

By Eugene E. Snyder

Binford & Mort Publishing
Portland, Oregon

Portland Potpourri: Art, Fountains, and Old Friends

Copyright © 1991 by Binford & Mort Publishing

All rights reserved. No part of this book may be reproduced in any form or by any electronic or mechanical means including information storage and retrieval systems without permission in writing from the publisher, except by a reviewer who may quote brief passages in a review.

Printed in the United States of America

Library of Congress Catalog Card Number: 91-76512

ISBN: 0-8323-0493-X (hardcover)
ISBN: 0-8323-0494-8 (softcover)

First Edition 1991

Contents

Preface

MOST OF THE STORIES in this book are about art works or landmarks easily seen in Portland. We pass some of them frequently, perhaps even daily; they may be so familiar that we hardly notice them. But I think that when you have read the details about them—and about the people who created them or donated them to the city—they will come alive for you. They certainly did for me.

In a few cases, the subject of the story is no longer visible—it has been erased by the restless hand of "Progress." But it is well remembered and it remains, I think, a part of Portland's living history.

Then there are some stories about people with unusual occupations. And there are interviews with artists who have left creative works for us to enjoy. In fact, about the only thing the stories in this book have in common (other than having come from the same typewriter) is that the subjects lend themselves to the "profile" style of treatment, which the author enjoys as a way of telling the city's history.

You may be surprised at the absence from this collection of any article about Portland's Skidmore Fountain, which, when it was put up in 1888, set a standard of excellence in this new western town. That fountain is still, perhaps, our pre-eminent piece of public art. But we have already published an entire book about the Skidmore Fountain: *Skidmore's Portland: His Fountain & Its Sculptor.*

Because many of the stories in this collection are about artists and their work, I should give some explanation of my interest in art. I grew up in a family where art was a continuing topic of discussion and where paintings were subjects of admiration, or, failing that, analysis. Artists were visitors and friends. My mother (Amanda Snyder) was a painter all her life and her brother, Jefferson Tester ("Uncle Jeff") was a successful artist in New York City. Though his Gramercy Park studio was far from Portland, it added romance to a youth's interest in art. Also, at home, the fragrance of oil pigment and turpentine was a pervasive perfume. So, in all those ways, the atmosphere was artistic.

It seemed inappropriate to encumber this text with footnotes, citing all references and sources. The facts are not in dispute, and also most people read books for *pleasure*, trusting the author to have done his research carefully. However, I have provided at the end of this book general information about sources for Portland history, and also some specific references to less well-known works.

I hope this book will stimulate your interest in Portland's history, art, and traditions, without a respect for which a city's mere location would hardly be more meaningful than the temporary campground of nomads.

Eugene Edmund Snyder
Summer Solstice, 1991

The Illustrations and the Artists

The cover, depicting the *Thompson Elk Fountain* shortly after it was put in place in 1900, is a watercolor painting by Oregon artist Clive Davies.

Ink drawings of The Elk (page 14), A Benson Fountain (page 17), Joy on Council Crest (page 31), Firemen's Memorial (page 44), Lone Fir Cemetery tombstones (pages 57 and 72), St. Mary's Tower (page 135), An 1885 Facade (page 147), and the Golden Steer (page 159) are by Patricia Ballard-Anderson.

Ink drawings of the Joan of Arc statue (page 93), No Bars on the Bears (page 119), The Rats' Banquet (page 176), and the Wordy Bird (page 181) are by Emily Maxwell.

Ink drawing of Johan Poulsen's Wooden Castle (page 151), is by Laurie Levich.

Linoleum cuts of A Spirit from the Dead (page 85) and The End of the Line (page 185) are by Sandra Lawrence Mattielli.

Map of the Lownsdale DLC (page 128) is by Katherine Cameron.

* * *

Credits for the photographs are given under Sources and Acknowlegments, pages 189–190.

The Elk and Chief Multnomah

A FOUNTAIN from which fresh Bull Run water flows continuously! That is the way reports of the day described the monument with its statue of an elk, on S.W. Main Street between 3rd and 4th Avenues, when it was placed there in 1900. It is shown in the illustration on the cover of this book. "Bull Run," incidentally, is the name of the lake and river which are the source of Portland's water, believed to be remarkably pure. The name was derived from some cattle which escaped from a pioneer wagon train and ran wild in that vicinity.

The Municipal Report for 1900 had this to say: "Our public–spirited citizen, D. P. Thompson, has erected and presented to the city a beautiful fountain. Its base and reservoir are of the finest granite, surmounted with a bronze figure of an elk, the whole typical of the conquest over wild nature by the forces of civilization."

We don't understand *exactly* what conquest that writer had in mind—perhaps the domestication of this elk? In any case, the life and adventures of the donor,

David P. Thompson in 1860 when he was 26 years old and a surveyor.

David P. Thompson, are in themselves examples of a more tangible conquest over nature. He was born in Cadiz, Ohio, and he earned his way to Oregon by driving a herd of sheep across the plains. He walked "every step of the way." That was in 1853, when he was 19 years old.

In Oregon, his rise was impressive, and symbolic of another kind of conquest—a socio–economic conquest—which the nineteenth century frontier offered to those with energy and enterprise. Mr. Thompson gave a candid account of those early days in an interview published in the *Oregonian* October 5, 1888 under this headline:

WOODCHOPPER TO BANKER

The introductory paragraph set the stage for the autobiographic reverie:

> Calling at the office of the Commercial National Bank a day or two since, a reporter found the president of the bank, Hon. D. P. Thompson, for a wonder, at leisure and ready for a chat. The reporter...asked Mr. T. how long ago it was since he came here.

Here is an abridgment of Mr. Thompson's lengthy reply:

> It is just 35 years the 12th of this month since I landed here, in company with a man named Coon Easter. We had our blankets with us and we went back about two blocks from the river and made our beds and slept under a big log, just about where this bank stands. It rained like blazes, but the log kept the rain off us and we slept very comfortably.
>
> The next morning, I went up to Oregon City, on a boat commanded by Capt. Dick Williams. When I landed there, I had not a quarter of a dollar. I had an order. . . on Col. John McCraken for $40, which I presented. The colonel was extremely polite, as he al-

ways was, but he had no ready money. I proposed to take half of the face of the order and finally got down to $2.50, but the colonel had no money.

I inquired how long he had been in Oregon City and he replied 'a year or two.' I told him that if I had been here that long and could not borrow money enough to cash an order, I would hang myself....

Things looked rather blue. So I walked up on the bluff and took a view of the city. There I met a stranger and asked him if he knew where I could get anything to do. He said he did not, and that he was looking for a job himself. I asked him if he had any money and he said, 'Not a cent.' He remarked that he knew a man at Canemah, Capt. John McClosky, who wanted 200 cords of wood cut. I inquired whether he had ever cut any wood and he replied, 'Not a cord.'

I said I had never cut any either, but we could take the job and get away with it if we had any tools. The stranger said he knew a fellow in town, Tom Charman, who could help us to get some tools.

We went down and saw Charman and he said he could get us an order for two axes, and we borrowed a crosscut saw and got...some provisions for which Charman went security, and with our blankets, tools and provisions on our backs, we struck out for the tall timber, six miles up the river, and sailed in.

We began in October and in February had the 200 cords of wood cut, and earned $400. We worked like the deuce all day and became quite expert wood cutters. We had a bed of fir twigs.

The reporter asked Mr. Thompson what became of his partner.

Oh, he is a prosperous farmer in Washington Territory; owns a fine farm opposite the mouth of the Sandy River. He has a lot of valuable real estate in Portland. His name is Van Vleet and he is one of the best men who ever lived, except as to politics, which, being Democtratic, are terrible.

Mr. Thompson, as will be seen, was very active in the Republican Party.

After that back–breaking beginning, Mr. Thompson became a surveyor. He did the survey work for the first railroad in Oregon, that around the Willamette River Falls at Oregon City. He was then appointed U.S. Deputy Surveyor. A biography in the *Oregonian* December 14, 1901 described this period of his career: "Mr. Thompson may properly be called the father of the U.S. surveys in the Northwest.... He took contracts all over the Northwest.... Many a tree in the mountain regions was marked by him. The sturdy frame he had inherited from his Scotch-Irish ancestry stood him well during his...surveying in all kinds of weather...."

In 1860, he was employed in Portland by Amos King, to survey a controversial line between the King and John Couch land claims. In 1861, then 27 years old, he married Mary Meldrum. During the Civil War, he was in the Oregon cavalry, rising to be a captain. In 1866, he was manager of the Oregon City Woolen Mills. Returning to surveying, he took a contract in 1869 to survey a military road from The Dalles to Fort Boise, Idaho.

His surveying work brought him a knowledge of business opportunities, and everything he could save he invested. He became interested in the construction of railroads and formed a company to build them. He became vice–president of the Oregon Railway & Navigation Co. In the late 1870s, he invested in the Sterling Mine in southern Oregon and, as a surveyor, designed a plan to bring water 23 miles over the mountains to use in working the mine. It was regarded at the time as a great engineering feat. Finally, as the ultimate stage of capital growth, he became a banker, and, at one time, was the president or director of 17 banks in the Northwest.

Concurrently will all these and other business activities, Mr. Thompson was active in politics, as one of Oregon's Republican leaders for more than 30 years. He was first elected to the state senate in 1866 and served several terms in the legislature—except for intervals when he was filling some other government position. For example, in 1874 he was named Governor of Idaho Territory. His political capabilities and party loyalty had come to the attention of the Republican administration of President Grant, perhaps through the intercession of Oregon's Republican U.S. Senator, John Mitchell.

After what may have been a somewhat bleak period, rusticating in Idaho territory, Mr. Thompson resigned that governorship in 1876 and came to Portland. Here, his talents were quickly recognized and he was elected mayor in June 1879. The vote shows the intimate and cozy size of the electorate in Portland at that time:

David Thompson, Republican 1404

Judge Wm. Strong, Democrat . . . . . .<u>1361</u>

Total Vote Cast 2765

In 1881 (because, as the Republican *Oregonian* expressed it, "his vigorous and efficient administration gave such general satisfaction") he was re-elected.

In 1882, while he was mayor (that was only a part-time office in those days), Mr. Thompson and some partners bought, from the estate of William Irving, 288 acres which they platted as part of the "Irvington" subdivision.

During these years, his banking interests continued to flourish and Mr. Thompson had become a millionaire. It was, in the late nineteenth century, almost a ritual for wealthy Americans to make the Grand Tour of Europe. In 1887, Mr. Thompson and his family left on a journey to Britain, Italy, Turkey, and Egypt. They were back in Portland in July 1888, accompanied by many large crates of trophies. An item in the *Oregonian* July 31, 1888 sheds a pleasant light on that trip and also on Mr. Thompson's personality.

THOMPSON GROWS ENTHUSIASTIC

A reporter, strolling into the office of the Commercial National Bank yesterday...found Hon. D. P. Thompson superintending the hanging on the walls of a lot of magnificent photographs which he collected during his recent Grand Tour.

Seizing a long stick, Mr. Thompson began in the style of a first–class lecturer to explain the various pictures. "This," said he, "is a view of Jerusalem," and then he pointed out more places of interest around the famed city than ever the reporter heard of before.

Passing to a second picture, he continued, "This is the ruins of the great temple on the island of Phila, on the upper Nile.... This," continued Mr. Thompson, swinging his pointer, "is a view of St. Peters.... This," he continued, warming to his work, "is the Roman Forum...."

When asked why he did not ornament his residence with these pictures, Mr. Thompson said he had 600 more at home, and a lot of statuary coming. This collection is well worth looking at, especially when Mr. Thompson has time to act as lecturer.

In November 1892, Mr. Thompson was appointed Ambassador to Turkey. He was recommended by Oregon's two Republican senators, John Mitchell and Joseph Dolph. This was a "lame-duck" appointment. The Republican President Benjamin Harrison, running for re-election just a few days before the Thompson appointment, had been defeated by the Democrat, Grover Cleveland. Mr. Cleveland would take office in March 1893 and there would be, of course, a clean sweep of all appointed Republicans, to be replaced by Democrats. Even so, it was an agreeable honor, "one of the most important and desirable" which the President could give, as the *Oregonian* described it. The newspaper added that Mr. Thompson "will without doubt fill the position of Envoy Extraordinary and Minister Plenipotentiary to the Ottoman government with credit to himself and the government he represents. No man in the state, perhaps, is better known to old residents than Mr. Thompson and no man stands higher for honesty and integrity."

Ambassador Thompson left Portland November 22, 1892 by train for Washington D.C., and sailed from New York December 3rd on the Cunard liner *Umbria*, en route to Constantinople. He was back in Portland the following year.

Mr. Thompson was the owner of the New Market Theater Block, and his office was in that building. There, he carried on his many interests, partly in business and also as a director of Portland Public Schools and as a regent of the University of Oregon. One day in 1899, when he was looking at the *Skidmore Fountain*, visible just below his office, he was inspired to write the following letter to city officials:

> From my office window, I have an opportunity to see the great benefit The Skidmore Fountain is to Portland, by furnishing water for the dumb animals and birds, to quench their thirst, as well as the great number of human beings who also drink of the pure water which flows from this fountain.
>
> Nothing has been done by any of our citizens which has been of so much benefit to the dumb animals, and consequently to humanity, as the construction of this fountain, from funds provided by our late fellow citizen, Stephen G. Skidmore.

Mr. Thompson went on, in his letter to city officials, to complain that the city was neglecting the fountain and not keeping it clean.

"The dumb animals," which Mr. Thompson emphasized so strongly in his letter, was the phrase of the day for horses, whose muscles moved practically everything that did move.

It was the *Skidmore Fountain*, which he saw daily from his office, that led Mr. Thompson himself to donate funds to the city for a fountain. "The Thompson Elk" is the result. It cost him $20,000.

Even after the *Thompson Elk Fountain* was put in place in 1900, there was anxious concern for the "dumb animals" and their need for water. In the *Oregonian* of August 12, 1906, W. T. Shanahan, of the Oregon Humane Society, observed that "There are only three drinking fountains between the City Park [now called Washington Park] and the river where horses can be watered, a condition which is cruel.... In the warehouse district, unless the driver takes the time to go over to First and Ankeny [the Skidmore Fountain], the poor horses have to go without water."

The sculptor selected by Mr. Thompson to do his fountain statue was Roland Hinton Perry. He was born in New York City in 1870. He was one of those fortunate people who find their vocations early in life; he entered the N.Y. Art Students' League when he was 16 years old and, at 19, went to Paris to study. One of his first commissions was for the *Fountain of Neptune*, a spectacular work in front of the Library of Congress in Washington, D.C. In his sculptures, he often sought to achieve a dramatic effect. Sometimes, according to art critics, he did this by exaggerating nature—for example, by an emphatic treatment of muscles to suggest vigor. In the case of our elk, which he made when he was 30 years old, there seems to

These two photographs, taken at about the time (1900) when the Thompson Elk Fountain was put up, show the city's motive machines— horses. Their need for drinking water was a concern to kind-hearted

be no such distortion. One observer said the elk "satisfies the eye of the nature lover as much as it delights the artistic connoisseur."

Sculptor Perry made the plaster model of the elk in his New York City studio and it was cast in New York by the Henry Bonnard Bronze Co. The stone base, of eastern granite, was designed by H. G. Wright, a Portland stone contractor, who assembled the fountain and placed the statue. The work was completed in the summer of 1900.

On September 6, 1900, an enterprising local artisan submitted to the city council a proposal to wire the antlers of the elk and ornament them with electric lights. He offered to do the job for $30. The council referred the proposition to the committee on parks, where, mercifully, it vanished.

Mr. Thompson was satisfied with the appearance of his gift, and on November 29, 1900 wrote a note to the

citizens like Mr. Thompson, whose fountain provided horse troughs. The picture on the left was taken at Front and Stark Streets, looking south. The picture above was taken at First and Washington Streets, looking north.

mayor and council commenting on the fountain and statue:

It is believed by those competent to judge
such work to be as strong and durable as it
can be made, and should be as lasting as the
City of Portland. I only ask that you arrange
to keep the same clean.

David Thompson died December 14, 1901, aged 67. By his will, he left most of his estate to his son Ralph. Among many other bequests were these:

To his wife Mary, "all my household goods, pictures, piano, and all other musical instruments."

To his son-in-law Joseph Teal, $10,000 "plus my gold-headed cane."

To his granddaughter, Ruth Teal, "the decorations given me by his Majesty the Sultan of Turkey."

In 1902, his widow and children donated to the city funds for another statue. It stands in Washington Park and shows two Indians watching the *Coming of the White Man*. One of the figures represents "Multnomah", Chief of the Multnomah Tribe who lived hereabouts. The other is a "brave" or scout, who is pointing toward the Columbia River, down which, we suppose, are coming the canoes of Lewis and Clark. As one would expect from popular tradition, the Chief is standing erect and noble, with folded arms and a mien expressing stolid haughtiness—with, in this case, just a touch of apprehension. He has a regal bearing and would probably use the royal "we." Standing on tiptoe to see over the treetops, he seems about to say, "We view this phenomenon with mixed feelings."

The statue was the conception of Hermon Atkins Mac-Neil, an American sculptor who was born in Massachusetts in 1866 and who died in 1947. He taught sculpture at Cornell University, then spent the years 1888–91 in Paris at the Ecole des Beaux Arts. He was at

The Coming of the White Man, *by sculptor Hermon MacNeil, 1904.*

Chicago in 1892 and 1893 making sculptures for the
Columbian Exposition. A group of Indians were at that
Exposition, to perform in "Buffalo Bill's Wild West Show,"
and they fascinated Sculptor MacNeil. For the next 12
years, Indians were the subjects of most of his sculptures.

It was during this period that the Thompson family gave him the commission for the Washington Park statue, and it was he who suggested the theme.

He made several trips to visit western Indian reservations, and worked on the Thompson statue for two years. In September 1904, he and his statue arrived in Portland. The *Oregonian* (October 5, 1904) reported that Sculptor MacNeil "has been engaged all this week in superintending the setting up of his masterpiece upon a knoll in the City Park.... The idea of the group, as explained by Mr. MacNeil to a reporter, is that the powerful Indian chief, Multnomah,...has heard that white men are coming down the river in canoes, and runs to the knoll...to see them." The reporter pointed out that the placing of the statue was timely and appropriate, since the following year (1905) there would be a celebration of the centennial of the coming of Lewis and Clark.

On October 6, 1904, "before several carriage loads of Portland's leading citizens," the statue was formally presented to the city by the family of David Thompson. If you visit this statue, you will see that the sculptor cut his signature into the bronze base: "H. A. MacNeil Sc. 04." By 1910, Sculptor MacNeil's "Indian Period" had closed, and thereafter he did portraiture and classical monuments. In 1916, he designed the new U.S. quarter—an eagle on one side and the Goddess of Liberty on the other. During 1915–1920, he did a *Judge Burke Memorial* for Seattle.

In gathering material for this story, we recently visited the Thompson elk. The elk stands on a large granite base, which bears this legend:

Presented to the City of Portland
by
DAVID P. THOMPSON
A.D. 1900

Around this base is a pool, from which water flows into four horse troughs. The monument is located in the center of the street, exactly where it was placed in 1900. From time to time, a suggestion is made that the elk should be moved to a different spot, but sentiment and tradition always triumph over the mutterings of traffic engineers.

The elk himself ("him" we are sure of because lady elks don't have antlers and the Thompson elk has magnificent ones) stands in a sort of heraldic pose — something like *passant regardant* but not quite. The nose is in the air, and there is an expression of camel–like disdain — provoked, no doubt, by the streams of automobiles on each side of him. The traffic would certainly inconvenience any "dumb animal" who might want to get a drink from one of the troughs. The elk seems, after almost a century in this posture, to have become effete, but still alert to danger. His is the sad and lofty pride of an impoverished aristocrat. If he were among the animals on a merry–go–round, few children would elect to ride him. Despite all this, the monument evokes a relaxing calm and a pleasant wistfulness — like a Strauss waltz heard softly in the distance, far away.

Simon Benson's Fountains

WHEN YOU BEND OVER for a drink from one of Portland's familiar bronze fountains, do you recognize this as an alternative to having a beer in a tavern? It was the idea of Simon Benson, a millionaire timber operator, that his loggers would stay out of saloons if they could get drinks of water from public fountains. So, in 1912, he bought and paid for the installation of 20 "fountains, multi-nozzle, bronze, bubbling."

A member of the Water Board, commenting on the gift, said, "It is an act such as makes one happy."

In a ceremony at the time of the installation of the first fountain, the Superintendent of the Water Department said Mr. Benson felt that "thousands of men are tempted to go into saloons for a drink when, were it possible for them to get Bull Run water from a public fountain on the sidewalk, they would gladly do so."

Mr. Benson, discussing his gift a few years later, said, "One of the troubles I had in my logging camps was the Monday hangovers from weekend drunks." [Not Mr. Benson's, but those of his sawyers!] "And, if a stranger happened to be in Portland and wanted a drink, about the only place he could get it was in a saloon. Saloons were parasites on legitimate industry. I decided to put in drinking fountains all over Portland."

Even so, the proliferation and apparent prosperity of Portland pubs suggests that there are some people who think water, however pure, is not quite the same.

To design the fountains, which have a graceful simplicity with just enough embellishment to be pleasing, Mr. Benson employed Albert E. Doyle, a prominent Portland architect. Mr. Doyle was the architect for many noteworthy structures, including the original Reed College buildings (1912), the Central Library (1912), the U.S. National Bank building at S.W. 6th and Stark Street (1917), and Multnomah Falls Lodge (1925).

The *Oregonian*, June 18, 1912, reported that the first fountain had been placed at 5th and Washington Street and the second at the Union Depot. They were installed in time for that year's Rose Festival.

> Pedestrians are enjoying the beautiful drinking fountains presented to the city by Simon Benson, a wealthy lumber dealer. The hot weather has made them popular to such an extent that all four of the spouts... are often busy at one time.... The new fountains are bronze works of art....

After the first four months of their use, the *Journal* (October 12, 1912) printed a review of the fountains' success, with these remarks:

> Beautiful Benson fountains prove extremely popular... Portlanders take 100,000 drinks daily from them... delicious, pure mountain water on Portland's downtown street corners from beautiful and absolutely sanitary fountains....

At that time, nineteen fountains had been installed (three on the East Side and sixteen on the West Side) and the 20th was to be placed soon at the west end of the Broadway Bridge. By 1916, it was reported that the fountains "have advanced rapidly in popularity as the public has become accustomed to their use, and the 'drink habit' is now common to all classes."

The Benson fountains were only one of Mr. Benson's philanthropic gestures, all of which were motivated by a social philosophy which he expressed this way: "No rich man has the right to die and not leave part of his money to the public and for public good."

"However," added Mr. Benson, "I wanted the fun of spending my money for the public good while I was alive. I invested about a quarter of a million dollars in good roads and public parks. I spent a hundred thousand in building Benson Polytechnic School. I put ten thousand into the Benson fountains and another ten thousand in a loan to help worthy students."

His Benson Polytechnic School is now called Benson High School. He presented his $100,000 gift to the Portland Board of School Directors in 1915, for construction of a building to house a trade school. Mr. Benson's gift was matched by a similar amount provided by the school board. The first unit of the brick building was opened in 1917. That was in the midst of World War I, and during 1917-1918 the building was used for training soldiers. In 1919, the completed structure opened as a technological high school for boys.

His reasons for founding Benson Polytechnic reveal the self-reliance which is characteristic of the pioneer that he was: "I put my money in Benson Polytechnic School because if a person has a trade, he can become a self-supporting and self-respecting citizen... What this country needs is producers, not parasites."

In a more commercial venture, Mr. Benson built the Benson Hotel, which cost him more that $100,000. The commission to design it was given to architect Albert Doyle in 1911. Construction began in 1912 and it was opened in 1913. For his hotel, Mr. Benson found a gourmet chef, Henry Thiele, who later became Portland's most prominent restaurateur.

During Mr. Benson's philanthropic years, the Columbia River Highway was being built and he supported it enthusiastically. For example, he gave $10,000 to pay for construction of the road around a difficult rock face near Hood River.

Mr. Benson felt that some of his other investments, while not purely philanthropic, were primarily in the public interest. He put up $250,000 for the Columbia Gorge Hotel, near Hood River, "to encourage tourist travel." He selected the site himself. It opened in 1921. Chef Henry Thiele was temporarily transferred there from the Benson Hotel, as an introductory attraction. But despite efforts to promote it, the Columbia Gorge Hotel was a venture—perhaps Mr. Benson's only one—which was not entirely successful. After years of difficulties, it was bought by the Neighbors of Woodcraft to be used as a retirement home. About 15 years later, it was sold again, and re-opened in 1979 as "an elegant country inn." But three years later it was in bankruptcy and was auctioned off at a sheriff's sale. It is now open again, as a hotel and restaurant, and seems, at last, to be justifying Mr. Benson's vision.

Simon Benson was born Simon Bergersen, in a small Norwegian village called Gausdal, on September 9, 1851. Gausdal is near the town of Lillehammer, famous for skiing and winter sports. Simon came to America in 1867, with his parents and two brothers and two sisters. They traveled immediately from New York to Wisconsin, where two older children had preceded them. Simon, now 16, became a farm laborer. In 1875, at the age of 23, he married. In 1879, he, his wife, and infant son Amos came to Portland.

In Wisconsin, Simon changed his last name from Bergersen to Benson. To understand this, one must know the traditional style of naming people in Scandinavia. Simon's father had been Berger Iversen. When he had a son (our Simon), the son became Simon, son of Berger, that is Simon Bergersen. Simon's son Amos would have been Amos Simonsen. Simon's daughter Alice would have been Alice, daughter of Simon, that is Alice Simondatter. The system was simple and homey. There was no continuing family name going back to earlier generations. Each human being was a distinct individual. In a household of two parents and a son and daughter, each one would have a different last name. But it was inconvenient in the modern world, with its love of census-taking, data-banks, and statistics. The Norwegian government, about 1880, outlawed that old-fashioned style of naming people, and decreed that everyone must have a family name which would be retained by following generations. It was a triumph for the statisticians!

At about that same time, our Simon adopted the name Benson, as being easier than Bergersen to pronounce and spell in an English-speaking country, and all his children acquired the name Benson, too. Simon Benson, speaking of this, said, "I believe that foreigners who come to this country should simplify their names, for the sake of their children, and that they should become Americans not only in name but in heart also. They should learn to read and write in the tongue of their adopted country as soon as possible."

When Simon arrived in Oregon in 1879, he found a job as a logger. After a year of hard work, he had saved enough money to go into business for himself. He bought a quarter-section of timberland, for $800. There were six million board feet of timber on those 160 acres. He borrowed money to hire a man and a team of oxen to help harvest it. He continued to buy tracts of forest, and from those small beginnings his operation grew into a vast timber enterprise, employing hundreds of workers. In 1891, he built what was believed to be the first railroad into timberland, to replace the slow-moving oxen. He also introduced steam donkey-engines, to drag logs out of the woods and load them onto railroad cars. He was an innovator, with the imagination to turn difficulties into opportunities.

Around the turn of the century, a great market for lumber developed in southern California, where there was a building boom. Mr. Benson built a sawmill at San Diego about 1906, but found it difficult to get logs from Oregon to that mill. Moving them by railroad was too expensive, so he devised a form of ocean-going raft consisting of an immense bundle of logs strapped together with chains. It was called the "Benson Deep Sea Raft." Many of these were towed from the Columbia River to California.

Mr. Benson died in August 1942. The obituaries stated that he was 90 years old, but his death was just one month before what would have been his 91st birthday. This has led to some confusion about the year of his birth, which some writers calculated simply by subtracting 90 from 1942, thereby deriving his birth year as 1852.

In retrospect, Simon Benson's life seems to embody the American ideal—the progression, by hard work, from poor immigrant to inventive, wealthy entrepreneur and public benefactor. And it is difficult to think of anyone else who has left in the Portland area as many pleasing and impressive structures and public gifts.

Saint with Sandals and Birds

ONE OF THE MOST delightful works of sculpture in all of Portland is also one of the least known or seen. Not that its location is private or hidden. But unlike most public art, it isn't on or adjacent to any heavily traveled thoroughfare. Rather, it sits peacefully in a little courtyard between two buildings in the Good Samaritan Hospital complex. The courtyard is on the north side of Northrup Street between 22nd and 23rd Avenues, and just west of Loveridge Hall, the dormitory for nursing students.

The subject is St. Francis. He is wearing sandals and the plain robe one associates with the religious order he founded. His hair is cut in a monastic style. He is seated

comfortably on a bench, and beside him are five large
birds. The birds are big, no question about that. To a
literal-minded spectator—a pour soul without poetry or
romance—the birds might seem enormous, even alarming! But St. Francis evidently sees nothing unusual about
their size. He is quite at ease, and his arms are around
them. We, too, after a first moment of surprise, accepted
the scene and its dimensions as quite normal. That is one
of the charms of the work.

Loveridge Hall, completed in 1966, was built with a
long-term federal loan from the Housing and Home
Finance Agency. The building cost $1.4 million, and the
loan contract provided that one percent could be used for
"fine art." The Good Samaritan Hospital Trustees
selected Berthold Schiwetz to do a sculpture. He was

chosen after the Trustees had seen photographs of other works by him, and after getting the opinion of Dr. Francis Newton, who was then director of the Portland Art Museum. Mr. Schiwetz had done many other works of public art, and also works for private collections.

Mr. Schiwetz made the sculpture, which he entitled *Saint Francis and His Friends*, in 1966 at his studio. At that time, he was living on an island off the coast of Georgia. The casting of his original model was done at a foundry in Florence, Italy. The completed bronze work was put in place at its present site in February 1967. Mr. Schiwetz was present for the ceremony, and he said he was pleased with the foundry's casting. The total cost of this work of art was $14,000, which included transportation from the Italian foundry and construction of its base in the courtyard.

Mr. Schiwetz, as quoted in an interview printed in the *Oregonian* (February 19, 1967), said he wanted "to use this man who loved animals and nature as a theme... I

have a little religious story in much of my work... In birds of this size, there is fantasy." And, he could have added, there is also a gentle, playful humor.

The sculptor also said, "I try to make birds more like personalities." In this he succeeded admirably; each of the five birds has a distinct and different character. They are of five different sizes and five different personalities. What species of birds are they? Crows? Seagulls? We don't know. Nor does it really matter. But each has a personality of its own. It's as if the Saint were sitting with five dogs—a spaniel, terrier, poodle, dachshund, and collie, for example. All dogs, but quite different.

Making the birds LARGE was an inspired idea. It enables St. Francis to show clearly his feelings for the birds, the feeling of Love which he personifies, by putting his arms around them. If the birds had been small, life-size robins, he would still be feeling that Love, and perhaps showing it by touching them with his fingertips, but the demonstration of it would not have been nearly so graphic and visible.

Peter Berthold Schiwetz was born in 1909 in Cuero, a small town in southeastern Texas, into what a biographer called "a solid, conservative German banking family." It was assumed he would go into the bank, and his father sent him to "Texas A and M" to study business administration. But "Tex," as he called himself and as he was called by all his friends, preferred to draw, paint, and make sculptures in plaster. The artistic genius surprises us by appearing unaccountably in unlikely places, and Tex perplexed his family by declining to become a bank teller. The family submitted some of Tex's work to an art teacher and asked if he should be taken seriously. The answer was "Yes!" and that started Tex on his career, which he pursued enthusiastically for the rest of his life.

He went to Cranbrook Academy of Art and studied there until World War II gave him what he called, with his characteristic good-naturedness and humor, "a round trip to Europe with the 95th Infantry Division." After the war, he returned to Cranbrook and studied under Carl Milles. Sculptor Milles took him to Italy, as his assistant. Later, Tex was called back to Cranbrook, where he was head of the sculpting department from 1956 to 1962. He then went back to Italy. He lived in Florence and worked at a famous foundry which did his castings. It was to this foundry that he sent his model for our *Saint Francis and His Friends*.

Tex came back to the U.S. in 1966 and lived for a year on Ossabaw Island, Georgia. He then moved to Michigan, where he had his last home and studio in what had been a vacant church. Its name had been "The Angel Makers Church!" Tex died there in 1971, at the age of 62. There was a memorial service at Christ Church, Cranbrook, and his body was buried in Texas.

All of Tex's sculptures have a warm and delightful humor, even when there is, implicitly, a profound philosophic message. He loved nature, and animals play a role in most of his work. An amiable hippopotamus! Neptune playing on a fish-skeleton harp! An angel dropping a flower to earth. A grasshopper on a blade of grass. A wolf in sheep's clothing. Jonah (with a somewhat bemused expression) in the mouth of the whale!

Tex loved the countryside, especially (as we would expect for a Texan) on warm, sunny days. After a drive into the country one day, he wrote to a friend these moving lines:

> When I see this I often wonder how God could possibly conceive of such beauty. I feel embarrassed when I think of myself trying to create anything worthy of looking at. But I will go on and hope that He will understand and accept my apologies for intruding.
>
> Tex

Joy on Council Crest

MOST PORTLAND HILLTOPS are decorated with radio and television antennas. On Council Crest, there is a more artistic work—a bronze statue with attached drinking fountains. It is the statue of a young woman holding upward, heavenward, in outstretched arms, her young child. She seems to be floating on tiptoe, and the impression is one of joyful lightness. Around the base of the statue are three drinking fountains, each set in a basin shaped like a lily. The basins are supported on thin flower-like stems of different heights, making the fountains convenient for both adults and children.

Funds for this statue were provided by the estate of Mr. and Mrs. George P. Laberee. Mr. Laberee died in 1944 and his wife Florence died in 1948. Their estate gave $6,000 to the city for the memorial. City officials selected Frederic Littman, a Portland sculptor, to design and make the statue. The work was completed in 1955, at a total cost of $6,700, and it was dedicated in 1956. Mr. Littman was then a teacher at the Portland Art Museum school.

During a visit to Mr. Littman's studio sometime after that, I asked him about the Council Crest statue. "I had great freedom with that work," he said. "Government projects are usually made under rather confining specifications. But that one was unrestricted."

Mr. Littman said the mother-and-child theme he chose has interested sculptors throughout the ages. He wanted, for that project, to make it joyous. Also, he designed the sculpture specifically to make the most of the qualities of metal. "I wanted the main characteristic of metal, that is, its tensile strength, to dominate. With metal, you can support a work off-balance with a small understructure. I tried to create motion by throwing it off-balance forward. The idea was to take advantage of the nature of the material."

Work on the project began in 1951 and extended over a period of four years. It was, of course, only one of many projects, besides his teaching, which occupied Mr. Littman during that time. But the design was perfected slowly, and the execution involved experimentation and contemplation.

The Council Crest statue is not a casting. Rather, it was made by working directly with the metal, by hammering and welding the bronze. Mr. Littman said he found the heavy sheet bronze interesting, but difficult to work with. It would not take a compound curve, so that he had to cut pieces for small areas and then weld them together. In some places, he built up the surface by melting drops of bronze rod onto it. Some of the pleasing surface effects from those melted drops, and also from the welding lines, "crept in. They weren't consciously planned."

"Bronze," he said, "has a lower melting point than steel, but it is difficult to weld. It is disobedient to the torch. It caves in. You might say it is fast and playful."

Frederic was born in Hungary in 1907. He went to Paris in the 1930s and was married there in 1940. He and his wife Marianne came to the United States later that year, and he taught art at Antioch College, in Ohio, from 1940 to 1941. In the fall of 1941, he came to Reed College as an art instructor. In 1946, he became a teacher at the Portland Art Museum school. He left there in 1961 to become Associate Professor of Art at Portland State University. He died in 1979, aged 72.

Mr. Littman's metal sculptures typically evoke an emotion of hopefulness and joy. He captured this in his Council Crest bronze by its impression of weightlessness. Despite its metallic substance, it seems to float as lightly as a large feather, appearing hardly to touch the earth. The metal's strength enabled him to support the figure almost entirely by its toes. As Mr. Littman expressed it, "I like to fight gravity."

There are many works by Mr. Littman in the Portland area. Several are readily visible, including these:

Copper Doors: Zion Lutheran Church, 1015 S.W. 18th., 1950.

Madonna and Child: a relief made of hammered lead, University of Portland, on a wall by the library, 1958.

Crucifix: Cast bronze, in the chapel at Gethsemeni Catholic Cemetery, 11666 S.E. Stevens Rd., 1964.

Farewell to Orpheus: Cast bronze, in a fountain in a Park Block at Portland State University, 1968.

The Flogger: Cast stainless steel, at ESCO, 2141 N.W. 25th. Mr. Littman made the plaster model in 1968. It was cast by ESCO (a foundry whose business is making castings) and dedicated in 1971. A flogger is the workman who, with a heavy sledge, breaks off from a casting the protuberances remaining from the tubes through which the molten metal was poured into the mold.

The fountain sculpture on Council Crest was dedicated without any specific name. That was a concern to Mr. Littman. He said, "People may start giving names to it." He had tried to decide on a title but had not settled on one. As he anticipated, various names have been given to his Council Crest figure. Among them are "The Laberee Memorial Fountain," "Mother and Child," "Pioneer Woman," and "Young Pioneer Woman." But such titles don't seem to describe the spirit of this work specifically. A title which I think *would* fit, and one which Mr. Littman might approve, is simply "JOY."

Firemen's Memorial

FIRE WAS RAGING in an oil company depot and warehouse on Portland's eastside waterfront between Salmon and Main Streets. It was a four-alarm conflagration, and around the burning building were many fire engines, some of them pulled by horses, for it was June 26, 1911. The streets were full of fire hoses and firemen, who were somewhat impeded by hundreds of spectators. It was a sensational fire, with the frequent roar and flash of exploding oil drums.

In command of the battle was the head of the fire department himself, Chief David Campbell. The chief was at one of the building's entrances, about to go inside to determine how best to subdue the flames. Close to Chief Campbell was Patrolman Evans, who laid a detaining hand upon the chief's arm and said, "Don't go in there, Chief—you'll get hurt sure." To which the chief gallantly replied, "I've got to—I've got to get in there where we can fight it." And he walked boldly into the building.

Shortly afterward, as a reporter described it in the next day's *Oregonian*, "A fearful explosion wrecked the one-story concrete structure. The chief was plunged to death in a seething cauldron, amid tons of debris." Hours later, his body was recovered; it was identified by some badly-burned gold buttons. He was 47 years old.

Chief Campbell was a popular man in Portland. He was born in Pittsburgh, Pennsylvania, March 10, 1864, and came here with his parents in 1878. In 1881, he started working as a fireman. He was 17 years old.

During the early 1880s, the city's firemen were making the transition from volunteers to paid employees. Theretofore, the fire engines, ladder trucks, and hose carts had been pulled by hand and operated by businessmen who volunteered for the duty. The various fire companies were like rather elite social clubs, and membership in them was a civic honor and privilege. But the equipment was becoming increasingly complicated and heavier. It became necessary to use horses to pull the engines, and the horses and machinery required full-time care. Gradually, paid employees replaced the volunteers, until all firemen were professionals. Dave Campbell was among the first hired employees. His assignment was to drive the hose cart attached to Engine Company No. 1, housed on Morrison Street between First and Second Streets.

Dave was a strong and athletic young man, and he was also at that time developing another interest—amateur boxing. Early in 1885, he proved himself adept with his fists by knocking out one "Jumbo" Reilly. Later that year, a famous fighter—the world middleweight champion—was in Portland. His name was Jack Dempsey. (This was *not* the Jack Dempsey some of us living today still remember, but an earlier fighter known as "the Nonpareil" — the unequaled!) Our later Jack, the heavyweight world champion, was really William Har-

David Campbell as a boxer. The photo was probably taken between 1885 and 1890, when he was in his 20s.

rison Dempsey, known to family and friends as "Harry." He was born in 1895, the same year that "Jack, the Nonpareil" died. It was years later that Harry Dempsey adopted the name "Jack" for prize ring purposes.

Dave Campbell was suggested as an opponent for the awesome "Nonpareil" and, far from being daunted, Dave accepted the chance eagerly. Jack and Dave faced each other in November 1885, in an improvised ring at a farm near the Lewis River, in what was then Washington Territory. The remote location was deemed advisable because prizefighting, with its attendant betting, could be a misdemeanor—a breach of the peace!—and the gendarmes might have interrupted the affair. The time and place of the engagement were passed in whispered words among the fans. By the day of the fight, however, it was hardly secret—steamboats ran special excursions from Portland to a landing near the site, across the Columbia River from St. Helens, Oregon. About 1,000 enthusiasts found their way to the spectacle. Among the crowd was at least one woman, who dressed in men's clothing in order to watch the fisticuffs. It was a bare-knuckle fight, which ended in the third round when Dave's nose was broken. Despite the outcome, Dave impressed the fans by his clever boxing.

Jack and Dave became good friends—boxing, after all, is a professional craft and opponents need feel no more personal animosity than two chess players. Jack took Dave "back East" with him, and they traveled around eastern cities giving sparring exhibitions. Dave then returned to Portland and the fire department. But he continued his interest in boxing. Backed by Dempsey and several other supporters, Dave was matched with the famous James J. Corbett in July 1889. This time, the promoters held the event in Portland. Perhaps they billed it as an "athletic exhibition" and promised not to cause a "breach of the peace." If, in this 1889 bout, Dave fought

Corbett as a heavyweight (175 pounds or more), he must have put on a little weight, because four years before he had fought Dempsey as a middleweight (160 to 174 pounds). The Campbell-Corbett fight lasted 10 rounds and Dave held Corbett to a draw. That was a noteworthy achievement in view of the fact that Corbett went on to win the world heavyweight championship three years later, defeating John L. Sullivan at New Orleans in 1892. (That Corbett-Sullivan bout was the first championship contest using big gloves—before that, the weapons had been bare knuckles.)

Meanwhile, Jack "the Nonpareil" Dempsey had made Portland his home. In 1886, he had married a Portland girl, Margaret Brady. But he continued his boxing career. Unfortunately, he came up against a fighter, Bob Fitzsimmons, who not only took the middleweight championship away from Jack but also knocked him about so severely that he was damaged permanently. That was in 1891. His health deteriorated and he died in 1895, aged 32. His body was buried in Mt. Calvary Cemetery. One of the pallbearers was Chief David Campbell.

When the Multnomah Amateur Athletic Club, organized in February 1891, decided to employ an instructor in "the manly art of self-defense," they hired Dave Campbell. We would think they could hardly have done better. Although he had already become a Battalion Chief in the fire department, he took on the extra-curricular activity and taught boxing at the Multnomah Club for about five years. When he was appointed Chief of the fire department in 1893, his official duties became more demanding and he was eventually obliged to resign from the boxing instructorship. The Multnomah Club, in those days, was located in a gym in "Columbia Hall," on Second Street.

Because of his varied activities, his kindness, and his pleasant personality, Dave Campbell made many friends.

When his funeral was held on June 28, 1911, following his death in the oil depot fire, it was attended by thousands of mourners. The hearse was drawn by the chief's three favorite fire horses, a team which he had driven himself in earlier days.

In a reminiscence (*Oregon Journal*, March 13, 1932) by a later head of the fire department, Chief Kerrigan, Dave Campbell's funeral was recalled:

> The chief was one of the most popular men in the city. For his funeral, the whole town turned out. It was the biggest funeral in the history of the city. Only Henry Weinhard's funeral could compare with it for floral tributes and the number of persons. They buried Dave from the Elks Club, then at Broadway and Stark. The cortege went up 4th. The sidewalks were not big enough to accomodate the people, and they swarmed into the streets.

The *Evening Telegram* suggested that a fund should be raised to pay for a memorial to Chief Campbell. The newspaper stated: "The thousands of friends...the chief had made in his veteran sevice have been so ineffably shocked and sorrow stricken over his untimely taking off that they have not had time to think of what they should do to assist in handing down his name to future generations as an inspiration to heroism and self-sacrifice..." The *Telegram* said it would receive contributions for such a memorial fund. One person sending in his contribution appended to his check a note stating that it was a tribute to Dave's having been "always on the aquare."

Long before the memorial was put up, another tribute, a namesake, was given Chief Campbell. In 1913, a new fireboat was launched, named the *David Campbell*.

His widow christened the boat, which, at the time, was considered to be the ultimate in fireboat sophistication.

Many years later, on June 28, 1928, seventeen years to the day after Chief Campbell's funeral, a Firemen's Memorial was unveiled. It is located in the triangular lot formed by West Burnside Street and S.W. 18th an 19th Avenues. The memorial consists of a stone terrace and a limestone cenotaph on which is a bronze bas-relief of Chief Campbell. It cost $35,000, which was raised by private contributions, particularly one very substantial gift by a donor who asked to remain anonymous.

The bas-relief, showing David Campbell in his uniform and holding his Chief's helmet in his hand, was done by Avard Tennyson Fairbanks. Mr. Fairbanks made the sculpture in 1927, when he was professor of sculpture at the University of Oregon. It was brought to Portland in 1928 and placed on the stone slab above the fountain and pool. Design of the memorial terrace, fountain, and pool was done by Ernest F. Tucker, Portland architect. At the unveiling ceremony, the memorial was described as "one of the finest works of art that the city has." Addresses were delivered by public officials and the Police Quartet sang.

Mr. Fairbanks also did the large bronze doors at the entrance to the U.S. National Bank, on S.W. Broadway at Stark Street. They are also in bas-relief and display a panorama of Oregon history. The sculptor modeled them in 1924 at the University of Oregon. The castings were made by the Oregon Brass Works and the doors were put in place in July 1925.

The Firemen's Memorial is not to Chief Campbell alone, but to all Portland firemen who have been or may be killed in the line of duty. There are 32 small brass plaques on the stone paving in front of the pool, showing the names of the 32 firemen who have been killed at fires throughout the city's history. By each man's name are dates showing the period during which he worked as a fireman. The first fireman killed in the performance of his duty was F. Wagner, who was a fireman from 1885 until his death in 1890. The latest was J. L. Devaney, a fireman from 1949 until his death in 1977.

Around the bas-relief is this legend: "Erected by many friends in honor of David Campbell." Below his portrait is this statement: "Chief of the Portland Fire Department 1893-1911, who lost his life in the performance of his duty June 26, 1911. Greater Love Hath No Man Than This."

Artist in Metal: Tom Hardy

QUITE UNLIKE the easel-pigment garret one associates with more conventional artists is the studio of a metal sculptor. It is full of rolls of wire, sheet metal, chunks of brass, welding apparatus, acetylene tanks, torches, hacksaws, and hammers. And yet, with equipment more suggestive of an automobile body shop than an artist's atelier, metal sculptors like Tom Hardy can produce work showing great analytical perception and sensitive treatment of subject matter.

Over the years, there have been many exhibitions of Mr. Hardy's delightful and imaginatively executed creations. At one of these, some time ago, the sculptor himself was present, to give a lecture, and I took the opportunity to ask him why metal appeals to him as an art medium.

"You can do things with it that you can't do with other materials," he said. "You can get massive areas. And you can do exciting things structurally. A heavy thing can be supported at a tiny point. And you can cantilever things, or build them up with planes of sheet metal."

Mr. Hardy explained that there are several different ways you can use metal to capture a subject. For ages, metal has been used "indirectly"—by modeling the object first in clay or plaster and then casting the form in metal. But it is "direct" sculpture—modeling the metal itself— that interests modern metal sculptors.

One way to do this is to build an enclosed form having the same shape as your subject. Or you can shape the metal with a hacksaw or file. These techniques reproduce the subject in metal, just as the traditional sculptor would reproduce it in clay or stone. But another approach, and one that particularly interests Mr. Hardy, is to "penetrate" the subject, to use space as well as surface. For example, you can "frame" the space with only "an outside line" of wire. A work of this kind was in the show. It was a cow, "framed" by lines formed by arcs of heavy wire.

Cow: *Welded steel wire, 30"x15"x8", 1953.*

Another method Mr. Hardy enjoys is to combine planes of metal with open space. An example is his sculpture called *Heifer*. It is made up of planes of sheet metal. *Heifer* is seven planes thick, with spaces between them. Battens separate and hold apart the metal sheets. In planning such a work, Mr. Hardy first make paper patterns of each metal plane, which he then uses to develop and arrange the composition.

Mr. Hardy's choice of subject matter—cows, horses, cranes, and the like—reveals the influence of his childhood on a farm. He was born in Redmond, Oregon, in 1921, and, as he put it, "I still have a little of the sagebrush in me." He can easily be inspired by the bony hip of an old cow.

"I think animals are more interesting than people. I mean, there's more variation, more decorative forms— the pattern on a lizard, for example. I like animals and their shapes as starting points, but I like to think a piece of sculpture is more important that simply a replica of the animal. It's a question of shapes, surfaces, planes, all interrelating."

"You mean it's the animal plus something of yourself?"

"Well, I don't know about that. It's nobody else, though," Mr. Hardy replied with a laugh.

A technique which Mr. Hardy likes is to lay brass on steel, in order to portray a surface texture or design. "First, you make a framework out of welded steel. Then you melt brass onto the steel. You use a welding torch in one hand and hold a brass rod in the other. You have to heat the steel almost to the flowing stage as you lay on the brass. Sometimes you get a snail-trail pattern in the line of the brass. You can go back and smooth it up by beating or grinding, if you want."

Each metal has its own properties, both good and bad features. "I like copper the best to work with. It's really reponsive. So is silver. They're both so malleable. But you can't get the wonderful strength you can get with steel. Also, copper is hard to control; when it melts, it seems to go all at once. But it gets a nice volcanic look from the oxidation."

"Would tin cans be any good?"

"Might be interesting. But it would be hard and very stiff. You can do wonderful things with sheet lead, though."

Mr. Hardy graduated from the University of Oregon in 1942, in general art. While a student, he was interested mostly in ceramics. He spent some time in the army, and afterward lived on a farm near Springfield, Oregon. There, he worked in ceramics and painting, particularly on nonobjective painting. In 1952, he received the master's degree in art from the University of Oregon. By that time, he was working chiefly on metal sculpture.

"Are the metal techniques for your kind of sculpture difficult to learn?"

"You can go down to a shipyard and see all the techniques I use," he said. "Someone once showed me how to weld. Took about an hour to learn all I need to know. I can lay a straight bead, as welders say, but I doubt that I could get a union card."

I recently asked Mr. Hardy which, among his sculptures in Portland, are his favorites. Here are seven that he likes particularly, with the location of the work and the date it was done:

Flight: Lloyd Center. 1961

Oregon Country: Portland State University (sculptured screens on a building along the Park Blocks), 1962.

Birds and Reeds: Lincoln High School, 1963.

Cranes: Holladay Park Hospital, 1970.

Badger: Wshington Park Zoo, 1976.

Running Horses: Pioneer Square, 1988.

Flying Together: Oregon Historical Society, 1990.

There are many other works in Portland by Mr. Hardy. They are easy to identify, because of his exquisite technique and his sensitive rendering of the spirit and feeling of the subject. It is a delight to come upon one unexpectedly. And when you see it, you will say at once, "THAT is a Tom Hardy!"

Eagle: *Ink drawing, 8"x5", by Tom Hardy, 1989.*

Foothills   C.E.Heaney

Charles Heaney and His Paintings

ONE OF PORTLAND'S best known artists was Charles Heaney. There were frequent exhibitions of his work here and elsewhere, and since his death in 1981 his paintings have become even more admired and sought after. Some of them can now be seen at Timberline Lodge and others are in the collections of the Portland and Seattle art museums, the Oregon Historical Society, the University of Oregon Art Museum, and in may private collections.

I often visited Mr. Heaney, at the studio in his home, to discuss his work and art in general. Once in particular, in 1956 when he was in a transitional period in his painting, I had a long talk with him. He was 59 years old, and very productive. Recollections of that interview help understand some aspects of his artistic career as well as some of the problems facing all painters. There was, at that time, an exhibition of twelve of his paintings at the Harvey Welch Gallery in Portland. They had all been done within the preceding year and they were especially interesting to those who had long been familiar with his work because they seemed to unveil a new period in his technique.

One apparent change was the brightening of his palette. I asked him about this change. He said he thought it was the result of his doing some of his paintings with casein (a water-soluble glue made from the curds of milk, to which color pigment is added). Casein, he said, seems naturally to suggest, even to call out for, more brilliance. Painting as he did in both casein and oil, he began to feel that his oil palette had been too grayed-down.

"The old ones are really way down there," he said, pointing to some of his paintings where the colors are subdued and earthy. "But there's a certain richness you get in a low, grayish key. And then, when you put an accent on it, that accent really sings out."

Several of the pictures in the show were in casein. But casein need not always be in a bright key, as was shown in a very appealing picture, done in a smooth, watery technique, called *Cowlitz River*.

In discussing the other paintings in the show, Mr. Heaney said he was a little uneasy about the one titled *Village Church*. "It's pretty sweet; perhaps too sweet," he said.

At that time, Mr. Heaney was spending half of his day painting and the other half as a jewelry engraver. His first art medium, which he began to explore before 1920 when he was still an apprentice engraver, was printmaking. Jewerly engraving, he explained, leads naturally to wood engraving, linoleum, and metal plates used to make prints.

The subject matter of a Heaney painting often reveals his great interest in the wide-open spaces. "They do think of me as a painter of Eastern Oregon!" And, he said, jewelry engraving may have been responsible for this characteristic. He explained it this way:

> "An engraver's sphere of influence is very small. He spends his time working inside a wedding ring with letters one-sixteenth of an inch high. Then, from 1929 to 1932, I had a job in the sign department of the Oregon State Motor Association. I worked in nearly all the counties of Eastern Oregon. That was the best job I've ever had for inspiration. After working as an engraver, with a magnifying lens, I felt like a man who had been looking through the wrong end of a telescope."

In Eastern Oregon, Mr. Heaney found a new world in that vast openness. From then on, he spent his summer holidays there or in northern Nevada, traveling by bus and making sketches for paintings.

Mr. Heaney said that the arrangement whereby he supports himself by half-time work as an engraver is a good one. "No one in town is making a living by art alone. Artists have to work at something else. Usually, that something is teaching. If you were, in fact, making a living by painting, that could be bad—you would always be looking over your shoulder to see how people were liking it. I'm very lucky to be able to make my living by something else. I don't have any restrictions or obligations."

Mr. Heaney enjoyed working out painting problems. He made many sketches of a subject, not to facilitate realism ("You don't want a literal representation; you would not be bringing anything of yourself into it."), but to help get the spirit of the subject. "I have to work at it. I'm not a facile painter. Out of five paintings, one may be a success. The others are scraped off."

In response to a question about his style of painting, he said, "I just paint. I'm not conscious of style. I just try this and that. I'm really not 'in style'—whatever that may mean at the moment."

A great many subjects always interested Mr. Heaney. While we talked, sitting in his kitchen or his studio, we were surrounded by many paintings, in various stages of completion and set up for leisurely study. There were the deserts and dusty villages, and a cluster of houses almost lost on a mountainside—slight evidences of human endeavor overtowered by imperturable nature. There were buildings in the process of being torn down—"Not that I like to see that, but it's interesting when that exposes their insides," explained Mr. Heaney. "But I often revert to the dry colors of Eastern Oregon."

Though his choice of subjects continued to be about the same as it had been in the past, the brighter palette seemed to make them less austere.

When asked about future interests or projects, Mr. Heaney said, "Painting is an emotional thing. It's not a matter of will. It's not like zoology; you can't plan a future campaign of analysis and dissection. I just work on a thing as long as the interest lasts."

Eastern Oregon Town   *by Charles Heaney*

Tombstones in Lone Fir Cemetery.

The *Gazelle* and Lone Fir Cemetery

BEFORE RECOUNTING the dramatic incident which is the subject of this story, we will set the stage for that tragedy by describing the way people traveled in the Willamette Valley in 1854. At that time, with no railroads and with roads that were simply wagon tracks, the Willamette River was the principal artery of travel. The falls in the river at Oregon City were an obstacle, but they were circumvented by a portage. Passengers from Portland and Milwaukie would come up to Oregon City by steamboat, ride in wagons around the falls, and board another steamboat to continue the journey to Salem, Corvallis, and other upper-river settlements. The starting point for this up-river traffic was Canemah (pronounced KaNAYmah), a landing about a half-mile above the falls. "Canemah" was derived from an Indian expression meaning "Place of the canoes." It was not until 1873 that locks were built around the falls, enabling a riverboat to go from Portland directly to Corvallis.

The Willamette River's first steamboats between Portland and Oregon City began operating in 1851. They included the *Hoosier No. 1*, the *Black Hawk*, and, shortly thereafter, the *Eagle*. By 1853, the Willamette Falls Transportation Company was operating a "through line of steamers" from Portland to Corvallis. The "line" consisted of the steamboat *Belle* from Portland to Oregon City, a wagon shuttle around the falls, and the steamboat *Oregon* from Canemah to Corvallis. Traffic was increasing, with the growth of population in the Oregon Territory, and the company decided to build an additional steamboat. She was launched January 18, 1854 at Linn City, a townsite (now called West Linn) just above the falls on the opposite side of the river from Oregon City. The Salem *Statesman* printed an account of the event:

> The new steamer...was launched about 4 o'clock. On account of the high stage of the river, it was considered best to have a steamer in readiness to haul her into the water, in case she did not gather impetus enough to run off from the ways herself, which was thought doubtful, from the fact that her stern was already in the stream and the ways covered by sand deposited by the high water. Nearly an hour before she slid into the water, her fastenings were cut and the props knocked out, but she did not move. The oil on the ways was so stiffened by the

cold, and there was so much sand on that part of them under water, that it was not without considerable difficulty that she was got off. But with the exertions of the gentlemen on the steamer *Oregon*, which tugged away at a cable attached to the new boat, she finally glided beautifully into the water, and was named by her builder, Capt. LeFevre, a gentleman of unsurpassed skill in this vocation, *Gazelle*. It was the common expression of all present that she is the best modeled boat in the Territory. It is expected that she will be ready to run in about 4 weeks. A goodly number were in attendance at the launch, particularly of ladies. She draws 8 inches, but with only part of her engines on board. Her length is 150 feet, with double engines of 4 foot stroke, two boilers 26 feet long, and side wheels 19 feet in diameter.

On Saturday, March 18, 1854, the *Gazelle* made her inaugural voyage, from Canemah to Salem. The *Statesman* was ecstatic about the new steamer:

ARRIVAL OF THE *GAZELLE*

This beautiful little river steamer arrived at our landing on Saturday last, about noon. This was her first trip, and she made it handsomely, bringing a large number of passengers and a heavy freight.

By invitation of her enterprising chief owner, Mr. Page, and her gentlemanly Captian Hereford, we went on board to dine at 5 o'clock P.M. Seated at the table of the elegant saloon of the *Gazelle* were some 50 Ladies and Gentlemen; all were politely entertained with a feast of *good things*.

The *Statesman's* scribe added: "The *Gazelle* is a beautiful model, and of the size and draught to be successful on the upper river. She sits like a duck on the water and moves like a thing of life."

All the next day, the *Gazelle* lay alongside the Salem landing. Nothing moved, because it was Sunday, and in those mid-Victorian days, the Sabbath was devoted to church, large family dinners, and rest. But Monday morning, March 20th, she was off, to continue her maiden voyage to Corvallis. She had on board a "pleasure party," consisting of "the beauty and chivalry" of Salem and Corvallis. The Salem *Statesman* was represented by L. F. Grover, the newspaper's associate editor, because Asahel Bush, the editor and publisher, was "temporarily absent in the States"—a phrase which reminds us that Oregon was still only a Territory. Mr. Grover wrote a mellifluous report, whose elegance may, perhaps, explain why he later became Governor and U.S. Senator. Here is his account:

> We willingly comply with a request to publish the proceedings of an *impromptu* meeting, held on board the new steamer *Gazelle*, on her first trip to Corvallis.
>
> It has seldom been our fortune to enjoy an excursion so eminently pleasant and satisfactory to all concerned, as the one in question; and it would be somewhat difficult to find anybody more peculiarly gifted with the qualities requisite to please and entertain guests, than the gentlemen named in the resolution.
>
> The party was accompanied by the Saxe Horn Band of Salem, who contributed very musically to the enlivenment and entertainment of the company.

Not the least interesting incident of the excursion was the marriage of Dr. E. C. Adair, of Polk County, to Miss Martha Kemp.... The ceremony was performed by Judge Terry, of Salem, who reflected much credit upon the whole bachelor fraternity by the circumspect manner in which he saluted the fair bride, after having securely tied the mystical knot.

The party was highly entertained with several Tyrolean songs by Mssrs. Bornhold and Klein, of Salem. Their parts were executed in a masterly manner and were loudly applauded.

We hope every member of the party may live to enjoy a thousand similar excursions.

The meeting, at which the Resolutions printed below were adopted, passed off with great *eclat* and the speeches were vehemently cheered.... These resolutions were adopted as indicative of the sentiments of the passengers:

That the guests on board of the steamer *Gazelle* tend to the owners and officers of the boat their most cordial thanks for the highly complimentary and generous entertainment given so freely on this occasion;

That the genuine urbanity of Mr. Page, the President of the company, and the gentlemanly conduct of Captain Hereford bestow the highest credit upon their successful efforts;

That the general cheerfulness and universal satisfaction exhibited on the part of the ladies is a certain indication of the continued popularity of the *Gazelle*, and it is our wish that the *Gazelle* may long continue to run....

Signed by 24 Ladies and 33 Gentlemen

> After the adjournment of that meeting, a spirited Women's Rights meeting was convened, the proceedings of which were not furnished to us, in consequence, it is presumed, of our being an anti-Women's Rights man.

Unless associate editor Grover was exaggerating, the maiden voyage of the *Gazelle* must have been the social highlight of the mid-Willamette Valley that spring.

Two days later, on Wednesday, March 22nd, the *Gazelle* was steaming down the river on her way back to Canemah. When Captain Hereford guided the vessel up to one of the riverbank landings, there was awaiting him a messanger, who had arrived by horseback, with fearful news: the *Oregon* had run into a snag, four miles below Salem, and was sinking. Here is the *Statesman's* account, published in the next issue of the weekly newspaper:

ACCIDENT TO STEAMER *OREGON*

> On last Wednesday, the steamer *Oregon*, bound up the river struck a submerged log, knocking a hole in her bow and opening her seams as far back as amidships. The captain and her crew went to work to save her, if possible, but all their efforts proved unsuccessful against the tide of water that rushed in through the breach and the gaping seams. She went down in 8 feet of water, lying considerably careened on one side. A messenger had been immediately dispatched for the Company's other steamer, *Gazelle*, to assist in unloading her before she sank. Captain Hereford of the *Gazelle* informs us that nearly all her freight has been saved.

It was later reported that no lives had been lost, but "attempts to raise the steamer *Oregon* have proved a failure. She will not hold together."

The *Gazelle* was now the company's only boat on the upper river. She was promoted with advertisements in the Territory's weekly newspapers:

Willamette Falls Transportation Co.

The Company's New and Splendid Steamer
GAZELLE

Capt. R. Hereford, will run as follows:
Leaving the company's warehouse at Oregon City Tuesday and Friday at 7 a.m. Returning, will leave Corvallis Monday and Thursday at 7 a.m., touching at all intermediate landings. Passengers will be taken from the Falls to Champoeg, $1; Salem, $2.50; Corvallis, $5. Meals will be charged for extra, $1 each. Freight, Portland to Corvallis, $20 per ton.

Though Mr. Page was the principal owner of the *Gazelle*, others had minority interests. Among them were Colburn Barrell and Crawford M. Dobbins, whose homes were at Portland. These two were also partners in ownership of a small boat on the lower river, running between Portland and Oregon City. Mr. Barrell was 30 years old and married; Crawford was an unmarried young man of 20.

Saturday, April 8, 1854, was a fine day, with no hint of tragedy in the spring air. The *Gazelle* was at Canemah, taking on cargo and passengers for the trip to Corvallis. She had been operating successfully for exactly three weeks, though not, it would seem, in strict adherence to the schedule announced in the advertisements. According to that schedule, she should have been, on a Saturday, up at Corvallis. Perhaps, now that the *Oregon* had been lost, the schedule of the *Gazelle* had been accelerated, and her crew had been urged to make haste! However that may be, it is certain that, at 6:45 that morning, she was at Canemah, amidst the bustling activity of imminent departure. Crawford Dobbins was on board, and Captain Hereford was blowing the ship's whistle, urging passengers to hurry aboard, because he was eager to get underway so as to make the run to Corvallis in daylight. The trip was only about 70 miles, but there would be several stops at landings along the way, and it was slow going against the river's current.

Suddenly, Captain Hereford saw his engineer, one Moses Tonie (spelled "Toner" and "Turner" in some accounts) rush up from the boiler room and leave the ship hastily. Accounts vary as to the engineer's behavior. According to one, he ran down the gangplank and hid in the nearby underbrush. Another reported that he ran off the ship and up Canemah's one street, apparently headed for distant places. A third stated that he jumped into a rowboat alongside the *Gazelle* and rowed frantically away!

We have no picture of the Gazelle, *because her life was so short. However, these two photographs give some idea of her appearance. The* Gazelle *was 150 feet long, the* Lot Witcomb *(right) was 160 feet, and the* Iris *(above) was 161 feet. All three had double*

The inconsistencies are an alarming commentary on the veracity of witnesses and the reliability of historical "facts." But all do agree on one thing: Engineer Tonie was in a very great hurry. Seconds after he left, there was a shattering explosion. The ship's boilers blew up, destroying the entire superstructure of the vessel. Steamboat explosions were not infrequent, but this was one of the worst in U.S. history—24 people were killed immediately and four more died from injuries.

The disaster was a challenge to Portland's newspapers. There were two: the *Oregonian* and the Oregon *Times*. Both were printed once a week, on Saturdays. They were small—one sheet of paper, printed on both sides and folded to make four tabloid-size pages. All the type was hand-set, letter by letter, and the printing was done on a hand press, one sheet at a time. Circulation was small—perhaps a hundred copies, or two hundred at most. (In an election in Portland that year, there were only 458 voters.)

Saturday morning, the printers were busy at the two shops when they heard about the explosion of the *Gazelle*.

engines, two boilers, and side wheels about 19 feet in diameter. The Lot Witcomb *was launched in December 1850, and the* Gazelle *in January 1854. The* Iris *was running on the Columbia River in the early 1860s.*

The word reached them via a riverboat which "arrived this morning with flags at half-mast, bringing us the painfull intelligence that the steamer *Gazelle* had burst her boilers," as Editor Waterman of the *Times* expressed it. The editors at both papers stopped their printing and, in the remaining copies of their editions, inserted brief paragraphs under large-type headlines. This was probably the first instance in Oregon journalism of a "Stop Press" edition. Editor Dryer, of the *Oregonian*, wrote:

TERRIBLE ACCIDENT ! ! !

After a portion of our edition had been worked off this morning, the startling news reached our city of the explosion of the Willamette Falls Company's new steamer *Gazelle*. We stopped the press, and despatched a messenger to the scene of this melancholy disaster.... Our reporter gathered the following facts: The *Gazelle*... had just landed at Canemah at 15 minutes before 7 when a terrible explosion of her boilers took place, blowing up her upper works, cabin, and after part, which were literally torn to pieces.

There followed a list of the names of some of the "over 20 killed and 25 wounded." Editor Dryer didn't state how his reporter traveled to Oregon City, a distance of about 15 miles. Either on horseback or by riverboat, the trip there and back would have taken at least three hours.

More details, and comments, were added in their next issues, a week later. ("News" moved at a leisurely pace in 1854; there was none of today's frenetic urgency.) Editor Dryer, on April 15th, wrote:

We have conversed with several persons acquainted with the circumstances attending the late explosion of the steamer *Gazelle*.... It seems to be the settled opinion of everybody, that this melancholy accident, which caused the most intense anquish in the hearts of hundreds of our citizens...was attributable to the reckless carelessness or incompetency of the engineer.... 24 human beings were in a moment hurried into eternity.... The engineer was permitted to escape and he has gone to parts unknown.... Human life should be held at a higher price, by those in whose hands it is placed on steamboats, than it now is.

Editor Waterman, in the *Times*, wrote:

The scene of the disaster, it is said, beggared description, and sickened the stoutest hearts.... It chills the warmest blood to contemplate such a scene. God grant that the re-enactment of such a catastrophe may never take place again. The causes are attributed to careless engineers!

The Salem *Statesman* printed an account of the tragedy but, since it was printed on Tuesdays, it was a few days late with the news:

On Saturday last...an awful explosion took place on board the Steamer *Gazelle* as she was lying at Canemah, with full steam up, for her up-river trip. There was a bursting of both boilers, with a tremendous crash carrying away everything above decks.... The spectacle is said to have been most shocking

—the shrieks of the living, the mangled
bodies of the dead, and the wreck of the
beautiful steamer, that in her death agonies
sent to their fatal end so many living and
hopeful human beings.

The *Statesman* had a correspondent at Canemah, C. P.
Culver. He wrote a report on the explosion, but it didn't
reach Salem until several days later, and was printed in the
issue of April 18th. It was dated "Oregon City, April 8":

One of the most heartrending calamities
that has, perhaps, ever occurred on the coast
of the Pacific happened at Canemah this
morning.... The new steamer *Gazelle*...while
lying alongside the wharf...at Canemah,
receiving freight and but a few minutes
before her intended departure for Corvallis,
was blown almost completely into atoms by
the explosion of her boilers.... The appearance
of the wreck is totally dreadful.... The details
I am utterly incapacitated to give, by the hor-
ror of the truly terrible scene.

Apparently, the *Statesman's* "man in Canemah" froze,
in the face of the biggest news story of the year! In those
days, it didn't really matter. Today, if such a one had
stayed in the newspaper game, he would have been taken
off "spot news" and assigned to book reviews, the church
beat, or articles on gardening.

The evening before the explosion of the *Gazelle*, there
was an eerie incident, which the *Oregonian* reported with
the heading "Singular Coincidence." Among those killed
that Saturday was David Page, the *Gazelle's* principal
owner. Friday evening, he remarked to a friend that it
was "just one year ago tomorrow" that he had put his wife

and child, both "bouyant with health," aboard the river-boat *Jenny Lind*. Shortly afterward, that riverboat's boiler exploded, and they were "mangled corpses." The next morning, just one year to the day from the death of his wife and child, he, too, was a mangled corpse, from the same cause!

Among the wounded was Crawford Dobbins, the partner of Mr. Barrell in riverboat ventures. Crawford was "badly injured." His left leg was "badly broken and amputated below the knee." Shortly afterward, he died.

Colburn Barrell buried the body of his young partner on a farm he owned near what is now S.E. Stark Street and 21st Avenue. His farm comprised 70 acres which had been part of the Seldon Murray Donation Land Claim. He also buried there the body of David P. Fuller, a Portlander who was killed in the same explosion. Most of the trees on the farm had been cut off, and the two graves were dug amidst "a wilderness of stumps," but not far from one solitary fir tree which had been left standing.

After these two burials, Mr. Barrell set aside 10 acres of his farm for a graveyard. He called it Mt. Crawford Cemetery, in honor of his partner. He bought adjoining land and added it to the cemetery. One deed (dated Portland, Oregon Territory, August 4, 1855) states that the land is to be used "for cemetery purposes forever." It became a popular burying ground for Portlanders, even though the mourners had to come across the river on a ferry boat to reach the still agricultural East Side. Sometimes the ferry would have to make several trips to transport a large retinue of mourners.

Mr. Barrell was one of the early settlers at Portland. He was born in Boston in 1824, and was among the first to go to California when the news of the gold discovery reached the East Coast. He left Boston in 1848 when he was 24 years old, and came by sailing ship around Cape Horn to San Francisco. He soon came up to the Portland townsite, arriving here in December 1849. In September 1853, he married Mrs. Aurelia Montgomery. She and her first husband had started across the plains in 1852, but he died on the trail to Oregon.

Mr. Barrell later changed the name of his graveyard to Lone Fir Cemetery. In 1866, he offered to sell it to the City of Portland for $4,000, but the city council decided it was too far away from the city's population. Later that year, three Portland businessmen formed a partnership and bought the cemetery. The trio were: B. P. Cardwell, a photographer; Levi Anderson, a Justice of the Peace; and Robert Pittock, a "provisioner" (dealer in wholesale and retail groceries) and brother of Henry Pittock, publisher of the *Oregonian*. They sold lots in the cemetery for $20 each. More trees were planted, so that the "Lone Fir" was no longer alone.

The earliest burials took place in the northwest part of the tract, where Mr. Barrell's farm was located. Later in the nineteenth century, Portland's Chinese community took a portion of land in the southwest corner, though the bones were sometimes disinterred and sent back to China for burial in ancestral graves. According to early caretakers, people from a wide variety of circumstances were buried in Lone Fir Cemetery. Several had been hanged. Some were gamblers or "girls from the North End," whose wooden headboards have long since rotted away.

While Lone Fir is the oldest existing graveyard in Portland, it is not the city's first. That was at what are now S.W. Third Avenue and Pine Street, where the building formerly known as the Multnomah Hotel now stands. In 1928, ownership and maintenance of Lone Fir Cemetery were assumed by Multnomah County. Today, with its many mature trees and shrubs, the cemetery is park-like. It extends from about 21st to 26th Avenues, and from Stark to Morrison Streets. More than 20,000 bodies have been buried there. The ground is pronounced admirable for a graveyard—high and well drained!

As for the explosion which started this chain of events, no conclusive decision was ever reached as to its cause. Jacob Kamm, who later became a prominent Portlander, was himself, in 1854, a riverboat engineer on the Willamette River, and he thought the boilers on the *Gazelle* might have been made of brittle, weak metal. Others thought the "water feed pump" (which forces water into the boiler—every steam boiler must have one) might have malfunctioned.

A Coroner's Jury was convened, which reached this verdict: that no blame lay upon Captain Hereford; that there was no reason to believe that the machinery or the boilers were in any respect imperfect; and that the explosion resulted from the gross culpable negligence of the engineer Moses Tonie, in knowingly carrying more steam than was safe, and neglecting to keep sufficient water in the boilers. They found that "the said Tonie" had escaped from the Territory and, though summoned to appear and testify before the jury, he refused to do so. The jurymen were unwilling to blame the assistant engineer, one Pascal Plant, since he was killed in the explosion, but they believed he was ignorant of his duty and too frightened to attend to it. The firemen were also killed. So there was no first-hand testimony from the engine room; the chief had fled and the rest were dead.

In retrospect, it seems probable that Moses Tonie, through inattention, had let the water level in the boilers run too low. When that happens, a phenomenon known as "flashing" occurs, when the little water remaining in the boiler suddenly and uncontrollably turns to steam. The engineer saw the pressure guage on his boilers going up fast and knew there was going to be an explosion before he could do anything to prevent it. No time to climb up to the pilot house and say, "Oh, Captain Hereford, may I have a word with you? There's something....!" He just got out of that boiler room as fast as he could—mortal fear being an overwhelming motivator. He was sometime later reported to be working around Puget Sound, but no attempt was made to extradite him back to Oregon City for a trial.

The Barrells continued to live close to Lone Fir Cemetery, on what is now S.E. 23rd Avenue. They had a family of four sons and two daughters. Mrs. Aurelia Montgomery Barrell died in 1899, aged 69. Colburn Barrell died in 1902, aged 78. During the three years after his wife's death, Mr. Barrell had, everyday, rain or shine, and right up to and including the day of his death, walked to Lone Fir Cemetery to visit the grave of his wife. He must also have seen occasionally the grave of his young partner, Crawford Dobbins, and thought of the *Gazelle*.

Tombstones in Lone Fir Cemetery.

Harvey Scott, by sculptor Gutzon Borglum. Standing at the base of the statue, to give a sense of scale, is your author.

Great Scott!
A Borglum on Mt. Tabor

EVERYONE KNOWS that Gutzon Borglum, America's large-scale sculptor, made the enormous carvings of presidents on Mt. Rushmore. Few, even among Portlanders, know that we have a Borglum here on our own Mt. Tabor. It is a statue of Harvey W. Scott, Oregon's famous editor.

Gutzon Borglum liked to think big. The faces of Presidents Washington, Jefferson, Lincoln, and Theodore Roosevelt on that mountainside in the Black Hills of South Dakota were said to be the largest sculptures ever attempted. Our Borgulm is big, too, though nothing like the colossal works on Mt. Rushmore. The Mt. Tabor statue, a full figure of Editor Scott, is only about three times life size. But it is placed on top of an eight-foot tall block of granite, so that the total effect is monumental. You will find it on the summit of Mt. Tabor, at the south end of the park. On its base is this memorial tribute:

```
┌─────────────────────────────────────┐
│                                     │
│          HARVEY W. SCOTT            │
│            1838 - 1910              │
│             PIONEER                 │
│             EDITOR                  │
│            PUBLISHER                │
│         MOLDER OF OPINION           │
│                                     │
└─────────────────────────────────────┘
```

Editor Scott, with his right arm extended, is pointing westward. Why he is doing this we can only conjecture, but it does remind us of another famous editor, Horace Greeley (1811-1872) who, with a similar gesture, said, "Go West, Young Man!" Our editor did just that.

Harvey Whitfield Scott was born on an Illinois farm in 1838 and spent his childhood working on that farm. In 1852, his father brought the family to Oregon. Here, in Yamhill County, they spent a year in pioneering farm work. They then moved to a farm on Puget Sound, near Olympia. In 1855-56, Harvey, aged 18, was a volunteer soldier in the Indian Wars. He also worked in logging camps. But these activities hardly satisfied his ambitions or his intellectual curiosity. Pacific University had been established at Forest Grove, and in 1857 Harvey went there to begin his education. He walked from the Puget Sound farm to Forest Grove, carrying on his back a heavy pack and, according to a biographer, "swimming the streams that crossed the trail." The largest such stream was, of course, the Columbia River, but surely he crossed that by the Switzler Ferry, which began operating between Fort Vancouver and the Oregon shore in 1846.

Harvey was in high school at Forest Grove for two years and then at the university for four years, graduating in 1863. He worked his way through those years of schooling by manual labor. His only capital was his good common sense—plus, it would appear from his career up to that time, a robust physique.

In 1864, he became a writer for the *Oregonian*, which was then owned by Henry Pittock. The young writer's literary abilities must have been apparent and impressive because, after just one year, he was made editor. He was 27 years old. He continued as editor of the *Oregonian* from then until his death in 1910, except for the years 1872-77. During that interval, he was U.S. Collector of Customs for the Port of Portland. He was appointed to that office during the administration of President Grant, a Republican. Editor Scott and the *Oregonian* were ardently Republican. In 1876, Mr. Scott was a delegate to the Republican National Convention.

When Mr. Scott left his editorial desk to concern himself with customs, Henry Pittock sold a controlling interest in the *Oregonian* to W. Lair Hill, who became editor. Then in 1877, when Mr. Scott left the customs job, he and Mr. Pittock bought back all outstanding shares, so that they together owned the newspaper entirely, and Mr. Scott resumed editorial charge.

He and the paper he edited from then until 1910 were intensely loyal to Oregon, and strongly patriotic. Editor Scott made the *Oregonian* a nationally-respected newspaper, and he came to be regarded as a principal spokesman for the West. His was the weapon that is said to be mightier than the sword—the pen!

And I do mean pen. He wrote out his editorials by hand. It is amusing to imagine how they may have been received in the composing room; his handwriting was not easy to read. It was flowing, eccentric, and highly individualistic. But, like that of every strong-willed character, it was consistent. Perhaps the compositors learned to read it as easily as they would read printing, so that they did not dread to receive copy from "the Old Man." That was what his staff called him. The term combined affection with a touch of awe, because Editor Scott could be autocratic and stern. But, according to a biographer, "His brusque manner was accompanied by the dignity and considerateness of the scholarly gentleman."

These were golden years for journalists. There were no rival electronic media, and "the power of the press" was overwhelming. Also, there was a romantic aura about newspaper work. The great short story "Gallegher," by Richard Harding Davis (1864-1916), captures some of the atmosphere. Editor Scott must surely have loved his profession. And, of course, in those days his paper really was THE OREGONIAN. It was entirely locally owned, and not a satellite of some New Jersey publishing chain. Nor was Portland a one-paper town; there were three or four dailies, all giving different points of view on public issues and competing to serve the readers.

During these years, Mr. Scott took and active part in political and civic affairs, and also in the Masonic Lodge. He was highly advanced in (it seems appropriate) the "Scottish Rite" branch of the Masonic fraternity.

Harvey Scott, editor of the Oregonian *for 40 years, until his death in 1910.*

His death in 1910 was unexpected, and associated with some surgery he had to undergo. He was 72 years old. He left his widow, Margaret, and three sons and one daughter.

Margaret Scott died in 1925. In her will, she provided $20,000 for a statue of Editor Scott, to be presented to the city and placed in a public park. The city council, in accepting the offer from her executors in 1928, designated Mt. Tabor as the site for the statue, that location having been recommended by the Art Commission. The sculptor chosen for the work was Gutzon Borglum. He was already well-known. In 1925, he had been given a federal grant and commission to do the group of faces of presidents on Mt. Rushmore. He was planning and beginning to do that work when he received the Scott commission. He completed his model for the Scott statue in 1930, the same year the first Mt. Rushmore face, that of Washington, was unveiled.

Gutzon Borglum was born on a farm in Idaho in 1867. His parents were immigrants from Denmark. The somewhat unusual family name derives, presumably, from the Danish word " borg," meaning "castle" or "fortress." The meaning of our subject's forename, Gutzon, has eluded all attempts at elucidation. His parents seem to have had a penchant for peculiar names. Gutzon's brother was Solon Hannibal Borglum, the significance of which is equally enigmatic. (Brother Solon was also a sculptor.)

Gutzon, in his 'teens, left the family farm and traveled to San Francisco to study art. In 1887, he went to Paris, where he was influenced by Rodin. In 1901, he moved to New York City, set up a studio, and devoted himself exclusively to sculpture. In 1904, he won a gold medal for a large work call *Mares of Diomedes*, a wild stampede of horses. It was bought by the Metropolitan Museum, and that purchase gave great impetus to his career. Among his many works were the figures of the *Twelve Apostles* for the Cathedral of St. John the Divine in New York City, and a large equestrian statue of General Sheridan in Washington, D.C. As his popular fame grew, so, apparently, did the size of the projects he planned. From a six-ton block of marble, he carved a gigantic head of Lincoln, now in the Capitol. His last and most ambitious undertaking was the group of presidential heads on Mt. Rushmore. After the head of Washington, that of Jefferson was unveiled in 1936, Lincoln in 1937, and Theodore Roosevelt in 1939. The finishing touches were put on the quartet by 1941, the year he died. This project was as much an engineering as a sculptural feat. Mr. Borglum had an assistant who was a structural engineer, and most of the modeling of the mountainside was actually done by local workmen using dynamite and jackhammers. For this reason, reference books sometimes identify Gutzon Borglum as an "American sculptor and engineer."

It was not until 1933 that the statue of Harvey Scott had been cast in bronze and received, with its granite base, in Portland. Dedication of the statue took place on Mt. Tabor July 22, 1933. Though 23 years had passed since the editor's death, he was still well-remembered, and a crowd of 3,000 attended the ceremony. Chairman of the dedication event was Oregon's governor, Julius L. Meier, sometime proprietor of Portland's Meier & Frank Co. There was a principal address by the editor of the *San Francisco Chronicle,* Chester Rowell. An invocation was given by Dr. J. Whitcomb Brougher, a famous Baptist preacher. Among our editor's descendants present at the ceremony was Miss Elizabeth Scott, who unveiled the statue of her grandfather.

Izquierdo Prints

MOST PEOPLE who know and admire the work of Manuel Izquierdo think of him as a sculptor. Certainly, his sculptures are well- known. Many are large and visible in public places. Among them are:

> *Girl Skipping Rope*: welded steel, Reed College, 1963.

> *Monument*: welded steel, first balcony foyer of the Civic Auditorium, 1965.

> *Campana* (Bell): painted welded steel, lobby of Lincoln Hall at Portland State University, 1974.

> *St. Paul*: bas-relief in wood, 1956 and *Pieta*: wood sculpture, 1976, Church of St. Philip Neri, S.E. Division at 18th.

> *Silver Dawn*: stainless steel, Wallace Park, at N.W. 25th and Raleigh Street, 1980.

> *Dreamer*: welded bronze, Pettygrove Park, near what would be S.W. 3rd and Mill Street, 1981.

Unfolding Rhythms: painted welded steel, in entry at 315 S.W. 5th Avenue, 1987.

Moon's Garden: welded bronze, in lobby at 1121 S.W. Salmon Street, 1989.

But Manuel has, throughout most of his artistic career, also made prints. I had seen some of them, and I became curious to know what role prints played in his creative activity, and how they related to his work as a sculptor. Manuel agreed, some time ago, to let me come to talk with him about his printmaking, and he graciously invited me to dinner. After a hearty meal of rabbit, prepared by the artist, fresh logs were thrown on the fire and we sat down for the interview. I wish I could reproduce his replies in the full flavor of his original delivery: a slight Spanish accent with a vigorous use of colloquial English.

I found that Manuel has very decided ideas about prints. For him, printmaking is a supplementary activity, almost a relaxation, from the media—stone and metal—with which he is primarily concerned. Thus he finds it strange that some artists set themselves up as printmakers exclusively. He himself turns to prints (he works on them in the evenings) as a kind of relief from the austerity of sculpture. The choice of subject matter is immediately wider, and all the "constructional" problems that limit sculpture disappear.

Because of the expensive processes involved, sculpture necessarily has a limited public. And, of course, there is usually only one occurrence of a work of sculpture, whereas multiple copies of a print can be issued. Prints, therefore, are for a wider public. In the best sense of the word, they are "popular." Part of the appeal they have for Manuel lies in this fact. There is none of the aloofness or privacy of sculpture. Hence the feelings which prints can best express are of a different order. Caricature and satire,

Woodcut
by Manuel Izquierdo.

Manuel would maintain, beg for paper. Acerbity and humor are given full play. One is reminded of Manuel's prints of various old women—he made almost a series of them years ago—dressed in fantastic furs and soiled velvet, the members of an outlandish aristocracy of their own.

As compared to sculpture, prints have bluntness and immediacy. For Manuel, prints are first of all black and white. Colors, at least as far as his own work is concerned, are out of place. He feels colors tend to introduce a "decorative" character. Manuel, in his prints, is seeking chiefly to make a statement, sometimes almost brutal, which can best be made in black and white.

Manuel's prints, nearly all of which are woodcuts, are strong statements, and can be strikingly stark. In the earlier years of his career, the flayed, dismembered hulks of war were often his subjects. These were, no doubt, inspired by his own childhood experiences. He was born in Spain and grew up during the Spanish Civil War. He left Spain when only a youth, and found refuge in France. He came to the U.S. in 1942 and to Portland in 1943. In 1944, Lloyd Reynolds, the Reed College professor, first introduced Manuel to the making of woodcuts. During the years 1945-50, he was an apprentice in sculpturing under Frederic Littman. In 1951, he graduated from the Portland Art Museum school. Since 1953, he has been a teacher at that school. He was also "artist in residence" at Reed College during the years 1954-56.

Manuel's major work continues to be his sculpture, but he carries on concurrently his interest in printmaking. "It's still a sideline, but I'm serious about it," he recently told me. He is seeking, as always, to achieve the harsh honesty which he values. Four of his prints were acquired by the Metropolitan Museum of Art in April 1991.

A Spirit from the Dead

AMONG OUR FAVORITE objects in the permanent collection of the Portland Art Museum is a carved wooden mask called *Spirit of a Dead Man*. It is displayed in a glass case in the "Northwest Coast Indian" gallery. This particular mask was made from yew wood by a Tlingit Indian who lived in the Alaska panhandle at Wrangell.

Its message is in its eyes. At first glance, the eyes seem to be closed. The lids are down. Wrinkles on the forehead stand out, and it is the face of a corpse. But look again, and behold! There are round, open eyes, subtly carved behind the lids. It is the spirit of that mortal man, looking directly at us.

Another look and the eyes seemed closed again. But we seem to see behind that dead face his living spirit, looking at us and trying, perhaps, to give us an intimation of immortality. That Tlingit craftsman was telling us something about his theological convictions.

U.S.S. Oregon. *The photograph was probably taken during her visit to Portland in June 1916.*

How FDR Scuttled Our Battleship

EVERY TIME I pass along Harbor Drive, at the foot of S.W. Pine Street, there comes over me a sad feeling of bereavement, mitigated partially by some pleasant memories. That's where the gray mast of the battleship *Oregon* stands, a faint vestige, a rather pathetic relic of the famous old "Bulldog of the Navy." The ship herself was tied up in the Portland harbor, as a historic memorial, for 18 years.

It was supposed, when the vessel was retired by the Navy and given to the State of Oregon in 1925, that she would remain here forever, a glorious floating museum. That assumption didn't reckon on the excesses of patriotic zeal during wartime. When World War II came along, she was taken back by the federal government, to be sold as scrap! It is a reminder, if anyone needed another reminder, that people do things in wartime they would never do in calmer, less emotional days. So in 1943, she was towed down the river, never to be seen in Portland again. But her main mast was taken off and left here, as a memorial remnant.

During the years from 1925 to 1943, every school child in the city must have visited the *Oregon* at least once. I remember a grade-school class tour—running up and down ladders; climbing inside the dark and tomb-like gun turrets; standing on the bridge and spinning the helm to guide her, in imagination, through treacherous shoals; admiring the beautiful woodwork in the officers' wardroom and the captain's stateroom. Then, down into the engine room—immense and mysterious machinery. Incidentally, the machinery had been eviscerated. Large chunks had been cut out; she could no longer move by her own power. The Navy performed that surgery when the ship was retired. The reason for that mutilation was the international "Limitation of Arms" conference of 1922, whereby the major powers agreed to hold their naval strength within certain limits. If the *Oregon* had remained functional, she would have had to be counted as part of our quota, even though technological improvements had made her obsolete. By making her powerless, the Navy was able to replace her with a more modern vessel and still let her live as a souvenir.

The U.S.S. *Oregon* was launched at a San Francisco shipyard in 1893 and commissioned in 1896. She carried 441 men, 32 officers, and 60 marines, in what must have been very crowded quarters.

In March 1898, when diplomatic relations between the U.S. and Spain were becoming tense because of a rebellion in Cuba, the *Oregon* was at Bremerton, Washington. War had not been declared, but, anticipating a possible need, the Navy ordered her to get to Key West, Florida, as fast as possible. She made the 15,000 miles, with a quick stop at San Francisco, in a little over two months, arriving at Key West May 23, 1896. She had to go around Cape Horn: the Panama Canal wasn't opened until 1914. War was declared on April 24th, when the *Oregon* was steaming along on her record-breaking run around South America. She was part of the U.S. fleet which destroyed Spain's West Indies navy at the Battle of Santiago, July 3, 1898.

In 1916 the *Oregon* visited Portland, for that year's Rose Festival. She arrived June 6th. The crew had a good time here, as evidenced by a warm-hearted letter of thanks they sent to the city. The original is in the City Archives. Here is the message, with its personalized spelling and style:

U.S.S. Oregon
June 12, 1916

Dear Mayor: —

We the men off the Oregon shure did have a swell time in your town, and we are writing you, to thank you for all your kind people you have got in Portland.

We would all like to visit Portland again soon and would like to stay there for a Militia training ship, and if you can get this boat, Please try will you?

We thank the P.R. & L. Co. for there kind permission of us to ride for free of charge.

Will close and many thanks, to you all, and all the People in your most beautiful town on the coast.

Your forever.
The U.S.S. Oregon, the
Bull Dog of the Navy

From all hands.

The reference was to Portland Railway Light & Power Co. (a predecessor of today's P.G.E. Co.) which operated the city's streetcars.

By World War I, the *Oregon* was already an outmoded vessel, as a result of technical progress. She spent that war in coastal defense and as a training ship, though not at Portland, as the crew had hoped.

Then came WWII. When it was proposed that the *Oregon* should be scrapped, there was, of course, an outcry from all those who loved the old ship and who liked historic remembrances. For those people, the amount of scrap metal involved seemed inconsequential in relation to the loss of this glorious memorial. On the other hand, the enthusiastic supporters of total war thought the sacrifice fully justified for the "march to victory!" The political clout of the two sides turned out to be about equal. The controversy moved up through the bureaucratic hierarchy. Bureaucrats don't like to make decisions where the opposing forces are equal; it's uncomfortable. The standard procedure in such a circumstance is to pass the problem along to the person next higher on the ladder, and let that one take the heat. And so it went. Finally, it reached the ultimate rung, from which there was no place to hand it on—the Oval Room at the White House. Sitting there was Franklin Roosevelt. One might have thought that FDR would opt for historic preservation. After all, his first connection with the federal government had been as Assistant Secretary of the Navy, to which office he had been appointed in 1913 by President Wilson. Also, he was a stamp-collector, suggesting a vein of sentimentality. But no! Under the pressures of wartime and the importunities of the advocates of all-out military production, his decision was to scrap the *Oregon*.

Perhaps, if the order had actually been carried out and she had been scrapped as intended, it would have been bearable—though sad and, some would have said, unnecessary. But, due to bureaucratic bungling, that didn't happen. The Navy sold the *Oregon* in 1943 to a ship dismantling company for $35,000. The company sold the guns, turrets, engines, boilers, pipes, generators and other equipment from the historic old ship. The company also removed the superstructure, which did go for scrap. But the great bulk of potential scrap metal was in the hull, which was still perfectly seaworthy. The company planned to sell that for $150,000 to a shipping company, which would use the hull as a barge. The dismantling company asserted that it had bought the *Oregon* from the Navy under a contract which allowed it (the company) to make whatever classifications it wished as to what was "salvage" and what was "scrap." But just then, in April 1944, the War Shipping Administration (a federal agency) decided it, too, would like to use the vessel for a barge. It informed the dismantling company that it was taking the vessel back. The company resisted, of course. The case went to the U.S. Court of Claims. After some legal argle-bargle, the court decided the federal government, under its wartime requisitioning powers, could repossess the hull but would have to pay $25,000 to the company for it.

The hull was towed to Guam and, during the remaining year of the war, our *Oregon* played the demeaning role of an ammunition barge. Thus, though we lost our historic old ship, she was never scrapped and used for war hardware as had been intended. What a pity we didn't have some national poet laureate like Oliver Wendell Holmes, who saved "Old Ironsides" (the U.S.S. *Constitution*) with his famous poem. You remember, it included these stirring lines:

> The harpies of the shore shall pluck
> the eagle of the sea!

If some versifier had tried to save the *Oregon*, he might have ended his paean with this little doggerel:

> The mongrels of the beach shall bite
> the Bulldog of the Sea!

But there was still one more act in this tragic-comic opera. When the war in the Pacific ended, the barge *Oregon* was tied up at Eniwetok, in the Marshall Islands. From there, in 1946, she was bought by a Japanese steel company and, at last, reduced to scrap. So we got our battleship back after all—in the form of Toyotas.

Joan, Teddy, George & Abe

SCENE I: The traffic round-about at N.E. Glisan Street and 39th Avenue in Portland. The proper and official name for that little park in the center of the intersection is, as we shall see, Coe Circle. In the middle of the Circle is a large statue of a horse. The horse is in the prancing mode, with two feet up in the air and two feet on the ground. On the horse is seated Joan of Arc. She is holding a battle pennant and is, apparently, about to trot triumphantly down 39th Avenue. She was placed in Coe Circle in 1924 and has been there since then, in a pose of suspended animation. On the base of the statue is this inscription:

JOAN OF ARC

MAID OF ORLEANS

1412-1431

Scene II: France in 1429, when Joan was earning her fame. At this point, dear reader, if you feel you already know enough about the history of Joan of Arc, you may skip to Scene III. For the rest of us, this following summary of events in France at the time of Joan's adventures will help us view our statue with greater understanding and appreciation. So now, to France!

A civil war is going on for possession of the French throne. The Valois family have been ruling since 1328, but their Charles VI (known, appropriately it would seem, as "Charles the Mad") died in 1422. They have not been able to crown his son, who would become Charles VII if they could perform the coronation. But a rival family, the Burgundians, claim *they* should have the crown. The Burgundian leader is "Philip the Good." He became Duke of Burgundy rather suddenly in 1419 when his father ("John the Fearless") was murdered by agents of the Valois.

One of the obstacles preventing the Valois from elevating their Crown Prince to King is that the French coronation must be held at Reims, in its beautiful Gothic cathedral. But Reims, and Paris, too, are held by the Burgundians. (Precedent must be followed as to the site of such formalities, if they are to be taken seriously, just as a British coronation must be in Westminster Abbey.)

Meanwhile, across the Channel in London sits the young English King Henry VI. We are well acquainted with his father, Henry V—who might be mistaken for Laurence Olivier. Henry V had brought an army across the Channel to assert some claims the English had on parts of France. He defeated the French in 1415 at the famous battle of Agincourt, because of the skill and strength of the English archers. It was a great victory, and Henry V—he was 28 years old at the time—returned to London in triumph. A song ("The Agincourt Song") was

written for the occasion. Here are its lyrics, in the original
medieval spelling:

> Owre Kynge went forth to Normandy
> With grace and myght of chyvalry.
> There, God for hym wrought mervelusly.
> Wherefore Englonde may calle and cry
> Deo gracias. [Thanks be to God]

But the victory was not quite the decisive event
protrayed, with pardonable poetic license, by
Shakespeare. The battles in France continued. In 1419,
Henry allied himself with the Burgundians. Then, in
1420, he made a treaty with the Valois whereby he acquired a wife. She was a princess of the House of Valois—
Katherine, sister of his enemy, the Crown Prince! Such
strategic marriages were not uncommon in feudal days. A
gallant knight might achieve before the matrimonial
altar a goal he had not been able to secure on the field of
battle.

Henry now had alliances with *both* sides in the
French civil war. It was his intention that he himself
should eventually be crowned King of France, thus unit-
ing England and France. But the fighting went on. Difficult to imagine how Katherine felt about it, with her
husband at war with her brother. Perhaps Henry ad-
dressed her as "My beauteous enemy!" In any case, it
didn't prevent their producing a son, born in 1421. But in
1422, at the battle of Vincennes, Henry died. The son, a
one-year-old baby half French and half English, was
crowned King Henry VI of England.

So now in 1429, under the eight-year-old Henry VI
and his advisers (the factious barons who are managing
the government), the English are in alliance with Burgundy, fighting the Valois, and hoping to confirm their
claims in France.

Onto this dramatic and dangerous stage there steps a young peasant girl. She is 17 years old and illiterate. But she is highly motivated. She claims that "divine voices" and visions from Heaven have ordered her to help defeat the English and Burgundians and put the Valois Crown Prince on the throne of France. These are days when many people are claiming to hear "voices" and see "visions." It is also the time of the Inquisition, and the Church is suspicious of messages allegedly from Heaven—unless authenticated, or received through orthodox channels. The messages may be diabolic, in which case the recipient may be a heretic or witch ... the likes of which, according to standard procedure of the day, should be burned at the stake.

Despite all this, Jeanne (for such was the girl's name in French, though in English "Joan" is closer to the French pronunciation) presents herself at the Valois court at Orleans. The journey itself is an adventure, because, from her home village of Domremy in Lorraine, she has to pass through the territory of the Burgundians. But the Valois courtiers rebuke her and the Crown Prince refuses to see her. She persists. Finally, they listen to her claim that she is ordained by God to lead their troops. The Crown Prince agrees—probably because they have been suffering defeats. We visualize the Crown Prince giving a Gallic shrug of the shoulders and saying, "Why not? What's to lose?" They put a suit of armor on her and hoist her up onto a horse—that armor is heavy! Well, whatever they might say about her visions, there can be no doubt about her courage. She plunges into the thick of it and leads the dispirited troops to a great victory. It is the Battle of Orleans, and she is thereafter known as "The Maid of Orleans."

More victories follow. They liberate (or capture?) Reims, and in July 1429 the Valois Prince is crowned

King Charles VII of France—though the Burgundians are not there to lay on hands and swear an oath of fealty.

The battles continue. Jeanne and her soldiers attack the Burgundian stronghold of Paris. But here, in 1430, Jeanne is wounded and captured. The Duke of Burgundy is not quite sure what to do with her. Her work against the English and Burgundians is well known. Perhaps she is just a POW. But the University of Paris, at that time the arbiter in matters concerning the Faith, insists that she be brought to trial as a heretic, because having communications directly with God is not orthodox. She is taken to Rouen, the capital of Normandy and a bastion of the English-Burgundian alliance. An ecclesiastical court tries her. They want her to renounce her claims about her "voices." They urge her to do that. They would like to let her off. But she refuses to deny her "voices." Finally, despairing, they condemn her as a heretic and turn her over to the civil authorities, who, in the year of Our Lord 1431, burn her at the stake.

Epilogue: Charles VII eventually makes a truce with Burgundy. In 1450, Charles enters Rouen, and the English retreat from that city and later from all of Normandy. Charles orders an inquiry into Jeanne's trial. The Arc family (that was Jeanne's family name) petition the Vatican for an investigation of the trial. In 1456, the verdict of "heretic" is revoked. She is, as we say today, rehabilitated. She becomes a national heroine and "The Maid of Orleans" is a potent symbol in awakening a French national consciousness. But that's not all. In 1920, 489 years after her death, she is canonized by Pope Benedict XV—made a Saint! From heretic to Saint!

Scene III: "Morningside Hospital," an insane asylum in east Portland owned and operated by Dr. Henry Waldo Coe. During the years 1922 to 1927, Dr. Coe gave to the city four large statues. They represent Theodore Roosevelt, Joan of Arc, George Washington, and Abraham

Dr. Henry Waldo Coe (1857-1927).

Lincoln. Coe Circle, where Joan of Arc sits astride her horse, was named for him.

Henry Coe was born in Wisconsin in 1857. In his medical work, he specialized in mental and nervous disorders. In the 1880s, he practiced in North Dakota. He became a friend of Theodore Roosevelt, who was there during 1884-86 to engage in ranching and to improve his health. "Teddy" and Dr. Coe were both in their late 20s at the time, and they went on hunting trips together.

Dr. Coe came to Oregon and, in 1889, he was practicing at "Coe's Sanitarium" in Portland. He was also professor of medicine at Willamette University. By 1900, he was operating the "Mt. Tabor Nervous Sanitarium," at S.E. Stark Street and 100th Avenue, in the suburban neighborhood known as "Russellville." By 1915, it had become "Morningside Hospital." It had more than 300 beds and was at one time the largest privately-owned insane asylum in the U.S. Dr. Coe had a long-standing contract with the federal government whereby mental patients from what was then the Alaska Territory were brought to Morningside Hospital. Dr. Coe had numerous other interests, too—in real estate and banking, for example. He was a member of the Progressive Businessmen's Club and the First Congregational Church.

On a visit to Paris, Dr. Coe saw, and was greatly impressed by, a statue of Jeanne d'Arc. It stands in the *Place des Pyramides*, near what is believed to be the spot where Jeanne was wounded in the battle to capture Paris in 1430. That statue was put in place in 1874, as which time it was unveiled by its sculptor, Emmanuel Fremiet. He was born in Paris in 1824 and died there in 1910. He is well known for his large-scale equestrian statues of historical figures. The Jeanne d'Arc statue is often cited as one of his best. According to art critics, his works show great attention to accurate detail, with a clear rendering of "the personalities of both rider and horse!"

Dr. Coe decided to have a reproduction of that statue made, and to present it to the city of Portland. It was possible to find the original molds from which the 1874 bronze casting had been made—probably covered with dust in the warehouse of some Parisian foundry. Other copies have been made, too: there is one in Melbourne, Australia.

Portland's reproduction was dedicated on Memorial Day, May 30, 1925, "in honor of the U.S. Doughboys" who fought in France in World War I. There was a patriotic ceremony, with bleacher seats set up for the spectators and the reading of congratulatory messages from President Coolidge and from Gaston Doumergue, President of France. (Aside: Perhaps our appreciation of the dedicatory context will be enhanced if we know the origin of the term "Doughboy." It comes from a small cake or cookie, about the size—hopefully not the consistency—of large brass buttons on military uniforms in the early nineteenth century. As a term for soldiers, it was well established by the time of the Civil War, and was very commonly used during World War I for the soldier known in later years as a "G.I.")

We visited the Joan of Arc statue recently and concluded that Monsieur Fremiet did capture Jeanne's personality, insofar as it is known to us from the preceding biographical sketch—proud, righteous, disdainful of danger. The horse's personality we know less well, but it seems to be a strong and worthy steed. You must visit the statue an judge for yourself. And you will notice on the base of the statue this one-line inscription:

A GIFT TO PORTLAND FROM HENRY WALDO COE M.D. 1924

That was the year in which Dr. Coe made the donation and also the year in which the statue arrived from France. The formal dedication took place in 1925.

Dr. Coe had previously given another statue to the city. This is the statue of his friend Theodore Roosevelt, located in Portland's downtown Park Blocks. It was dedicated November 11, 1922, and Dr. Coe paid $40,000 for it, a substantial sum in those less-inflated dollars. The sculptor was Alexander Phimister Proctor (1862-1950). His sculptures won awards at the Chicago Exposition of 1893 and at other Expositions in 1904 and 1915. Statues by him are in public parks in Pittsburgh, New York City, Denver, and Buffalo, and in the Metropolitan Museum of Art.

The statue of Theodore Roosevelt, with sculptor A. P. Proctor putting the finishing touches on his model, in his New York studio in 1922.

On the base of the statue is this inscription:

THEODORE ROOSEVELT

ROUGH RIDER

"Rough" is intended to describe the terrain, not his horsemanship! It is a reference to his career in the Spanish-American War in 1898. Colonel Roosevelt, then 39 years old, recruited the "First U.S. Volunteer Cavalry," known as the "Rough Riders." He led a charge against the Spanish in which he gave the famous cry (legendary but possibly apocryphal): "CHARGE! CHARGE THE BLOCKHOUSE!" The statue shows the "Rough Rider" in his cavalry colonel's uniform, but the modeling of his face seems to make him older than the 39 years he would have been at that time.

On the base of the statue is a bronze plaque with a tribute to Theodore Roosevelt. It states, in part:

> He was found faithful over a few things
> and was made ruler over many. He was frail;
> he made himself a tower of strength. He was
> timid; he made himself a tower of courage. He
> was a dreamer; he became one of the great
> doers of all time....

It is a eulogy that would be difficult to match.

Dr. Coe died in 1927, aged 70. He had gone to California for his health, and died in a sanitarium there. Before leaving Portland, he had given orders for two more statues: one of George Washington, and one of Abraham Lincoln.

George Washington is at N.E. Sandy Boulevard and 57th Avenue. It was dedicated on July 4, 1927. The sculptor, Pompeo Coppini, was born in Italy in 1870. When he was a young man, he emigrated to America, where he had a distinguished career as a sculptor.

George Washington, *by sculptor Pompeo Coppini, 1927.*

Abraham Lincoln is in the downtown Park Blocks. The statue was commissioned by Dr. Coe in 1926. It is signed on its bronze base:

GEORGE FITE WATERS   PARIS 1926

Sculptor Waters was born in San Francisco in 1894. After attending the Art Students' League in New York City, he went to Paris and studied under Rodin. He was living in Paris when he made the plaster model for the Abraham Lincoln statue, which was cast in bronze at a foundry in Paris. Shipping it to Portland and putting it in place on its base took some time, and it was not dedicated until October 5, 1928.

These four statues given to the city by Dr. Coe are conspicuous ingredients in our public heritage. And for anyone who grew up in Portland, they are as much a part of the memoried and enduring landscape as is Mt. Hood.

A Stroll through
Lownsdale Square

WOULD YOU LIKE to come with me for a leisure-ly walk through Lownsdale Square? We will see some of the sights and memorials that renown this city. Let's begin at the corner of S.W. 4th Avenue and Main Street. Immediately, our attention is attracted by a conspicuous object in the center of Main Street. We already know it well; the first article in this book described it—the Thompson Elk. To the south of the Elk is Chapman Square, another park block. These two Squares go back to the very beginning of Portland. The townsite's owners set them aside for parks in the original plat of December 1852. Later, there was some uncertainty about the city's title to the two "Plaza Blocks," as they were called. The city paid Mr. Chapman $1,200 for the title. The Squares are now named officially, one for Mr. Chapman and one for Daniel Lownsdale, another of the pioneer townsite owners.

But what do we see here in Lownsdale Square? In the middle of the Square is a tall monument, a very tall obelisk of granite on top of which is the statue of a soldier. The soldier is so high in the air that, with the Square's large and luxuriant trees in leaf, it is difficult to see him. That is unfortunate because the sculptor of this statue was, as we shall learn later, a gifted artist. We walk down the path that bisects the Square diagonally, to look more closely. On the west face of the pillar is this legend:

ERECTED BY THE CITIZENS OF OREGON TO THE DEAD OF THE SECOND OREGON UNITED STATES VOLUNTEER INFANTRY. ANNO DOMINI MDCCCCIV

So, 1904. But we don't recall any war in 1904. Then we see that the pillar is placed on three circular steps which bear the phrases "First in Guam," "First in the Philippines," and "First in Manila." And, looking up at the soldier's uniform, we see that he is dressed for the Spanish-American War, and carries a rifle of that vintage. The date, therefore, is a bit puzzling. Fortunately, however, I did some research in preparation for our outing. Let us interrupt our stroll, sit on a park bench, and review the history of this monument.

It is, indeed, a Spanish-American War Memorial. The Volunteers of the Second Oregon Infantry Regiment fought in several engagements in the Philippines, and the Oregon boys distinguished themselves. Harvey Scott, editor of the *Oregonian*, wrote a passionate plea for a monument to be put up to the "Second Oregon," especially to those of the regiment who had died. Editor Scott's patriotic zeal was mentioned earlier in the article about his statue on Mt. Tabor. His editorial of June 18, 1899 demonstrates that patriotism, and it is also a good example of his literary style.

Monument to Our Soldiers

A monument...is due to the soldiers of the Second Oregon who have fallen in the service of their country.... The monument should be placed in one of the public parks.... The best place, probably, would be one of the public squares near the Court House.... It should be built of granite, with large base, and on the face of the blocks around the four sides the names of the fallen soldiers should be cut with chisel, for preservation through the ages. The upper part should be completed after some appropriate design.... The spot through all time will be one of the shrines of the patriotism of our state....

Erection of such a monument will cost a considerable sum of money. The Oregonian wishes to make itself a medium through which the money may be obtained. The sum required will be at least $10,000, and perhaps might reach $20,000; The Oregonian will start the list with a subscription of $500.... The name of every person who subscribes, with the amount of contribution, will be published from day to day.... The question is, how can our people most appropriately honor the regiment and its dead.... Nothing could be so suitable as this historic monument...a daily reminder through all coming years of the gallant devotion and unselfish patriotism of the young men of Oregon who sprang to the front at their country's call.

The Oregonian appeals to the people of Oregon to send in their subscriptions.... The monument should be built this year.

Editor Scott seems to have been a man who, like Napoleon, believed in "quick decisions, followed by quick action." He wanted the monument made and in place by the time the troops got back to Oregon. His editorial appeared on June 18th, the troops returned to San Francisco less than a month later (July 13, 1899), and they were mustered out and back home before the end of August. Unfortunately, the memorial project moved

rather more slowly. Committees had to be set up, of
course. The chairman of the Citizens' Committee, which
managed the raising of funds, was Editor Scott. This
seems appropriate, since it was all his idea, including
the location of the monument and even to some extent
its design. Mr. Scott was able to report that, on the day
the troops landed at San Francisco, the fund had grown
to $5,780.

There was also a Construction Committee, its chairman being Colonel James Jackson, U.S. Army. Col.
Jackson conceived the idea of the figure of a soldier, in
an action pose, placed on top of the pillar. To make the
statue, the committee selected Douglas Tilden, who at
the time was, according to Lorado Taft in his *History of
American Sculpture* (1903), "the most eminent sculptor
of the Western Coast." He was born at Chico, California
in 1860. When he was five years old, he had scarlet
fever, which left him deaf. He was educated at the
Institute for the Deaf and Dumb at Berkeley, and
entered the University of California. Before graduating, he left the university to accept a position as teacher
at the San Francisco Art Institute. In 1885, his first
major scuptural work, *The Tired Wrestler*, won a prize.
He then studied at the National Academy of Design in
New York City. In 1887, he sailed for Europe and
studied and worked at sculpture in Paris until 1894. He
exhibited at the Paris Salon, and won recognition. From
1894 to 1900, he taught sculpture at the California
School of Design.

Among his works are *The Baseball Player*, *The Tired
Boxer*, a tumultuous group called *The Bear Hunt*, *The
Young Acrobat*, *The Football Players*, and a *Native Sons
Fountain* for San Francisco which was a column with a
miner at its base and a winged figure on the top of the
column. His works, as the preceding titles suggest, show
his interest in the physical strength of the body, with the

limbs and muscles in vigorous activity. Our Spanish-American War Veterans' monument committee could hardly have chosen a sculptor more suitable for the work envisaged — an infantryman in action.

A model of the proposed statue was in the hands of the Construction Committee by December 1903. This was progress, though it was already four years beyond the target date Editor Scott had proposed in his original editorial. Earlier that year, on March 5, 1903, the city council had passed an ordinance authorizing erection of the monument in Lownsdale Square. On the basis of these hopeful signs, the Construction Committee ordered the granite pillar which would support the statue of the soldier and also bear the explanatory legend.

It is at this point that we come into the realm of the unknown, or at least where we have to balance probabilities. The pillar clearly bears the date MDCCCCIV. Yet the granite base was not received from the Vermont stone works until October 1905, and it was May 30, 1906 (Memorial Day) when the monument was formally dedicated at an elaborate festivity. So why 1904? My guess is that the Construction Committee members were confident that everything would be in place and dedicatable in 1904, and ordered that date cut in the stone. Then—as will happen—delays obtruded; but the stone had already been cut. That is one possibility. Or perhaps 1904 is intended to show the year in which sculptor Tilden's model was cast in bronze? Another possibility—however remote—is that someone thought IV is Roman for 6. But surely..!

Despite this trivial and amusing peccadillo, the dedication ceremonies came off gloriously. The *Oregonian* of May 31, 1906 carried this headline and story:

THOUSANDS THRONG PLAZA

As the Stars and Stripes fell back from the volunteer memorial monument at Plaza Park yesterday afternoon, a bronze figure of heroic proportions, alert, vigorous, determined, was uncovered to the view of the waiting thousands.... The figure seemed to breathe and move. The face was thin and full of courage.... The gathering filled the entire block...an ocean of humanity.

Col. James Jackson, U.S. Army, was the first speaker. He said, "The sculptor of the figure is one whose artistic perceptions are both innate and cultivated."

Editor Scott spoke, reporting that the total amount raised had been $12,914, which had been augmented by interest received on the deposited funds and by a final contribution of $1,133 from the Woodmen of the World, so that the total available to the committee was $15,858. The cost of the monument, including the work around the circle on which it stands, had been $14,722. The balance, $1,136, was turned over to the mayor, for use in maintaining the monument. Included in the cost was the work of Horace G. Wright, a dealer in monuments and a representative of the Vermont Granite Company, who assembled the memorial and constructed its base.

This has been a rather long interpolation, but, of course, we have been sitting here on a park bench all the while. Now we shall walk around and inspect the monument more closely. Surrounding the monument itself are eight stone posts, apparently designed to imitate large artillery shells. At least, that is their shape. On them are chiseled the names of battle sites at which the Oregon Volunteer Infantrymen fought: Manila, Paco, Tondo, Mariquina, Guadalupe, Pasig, Laguna de Bay, Malabon,

Marilao, Bocaue, Malinta, San Ildefonso, San Isidro, Arayat, and Taytay. On the east face of the pillar are the names of the 64 men of the Second Oregon Regiment who died during the war. The Second Oregon was at full regimental strength, and numbered 1352 (56 officers and 1296 enlisted men). Of that number, 13 were killed in action, 3 died of wounds, and 3 were captured and killed, for a total of 19 combat deaths. Two others died from accidents. All the other deaths (43) were from disease, particularly tropical fevers and typhoid.

Next we see, on opposite sides of the base of the monument, two small cannon, or "howitzers." They were "used in the defense of Fort Sumpter 1861," and were gifts to the city from Colonel Henry E. Dosch (for whom our Dosch Road is named). Their history, and that of the Colonel himself, are colorful addenda to Lownsdale Square. Henry was born in Germany in 1841 and come to the U.S. in 1860. He enlisted (choosing the Union side) in the Fifth Missouri Cavalry, and rapidly rose in rank until, at the age of 22, he became a Colonel. When his enlistment expired, he walked across the plains, reaching Oregon in 1864. Here, he achieved business and social prominence—his title of "Colonel" must surely have been the opposite of a handicap. He represented the State of Oregon at Chicago's Columbian World Exposition in 1893. In 1901, he was in charge of Oregon's exhibits at an exposition in Charleston, South Carolina. While he was there, a party of army officers came to inspect the coast defenses and to make plans for the restoration of Fort Sumpter, at the enterance to Charleston harbor. The fort had remained in demolished condition since the Civil War. By coincidence, one of the officers was a good friend of Col. Dosch, having served with him in the Missouri Cavalry. Col. Dosch went with them to visit Fort Sumpter. While exploring the grounds, he found the two howitzers, half buried in the sand around the fort and exposed only at low tide. Col. Dosch, in a "Letter to the Editor" published in the *Oregonian* of January 27, 1906, wrote:

It occurred to me then to secure these howitzers for our soldiers' monument...the howitzers were dug up and...delivered to me at our [Oregon] exhibits, and at the close of the exposition we loaded them on our [railroad] cars and brought them here.

In his letter, the Colonel added that the howitzers were then in the rotunda of the City Hall, but that he had brought them back specifically to be placed by the soldiers' monument. At the time of his mission to Charleston, the monument was prominent in the local news, with Editor Scott trying to raise money for it.

Lest a Civil War monument from Fort Sumpter might create partisan resentment from any Southern sympathizers in Portland, Col. Dosch pointed out that the howitzers had been used by *both* sides in the Civil War. After they had captured Fort Sumpter, the Confederates loaded the howitzers on a barge which they used to defend the harbor from Yankee attacks. At the end of the war, they were dumped in the sand at the fort.

But there is more in Lownsdale Square—yet another memorial to Spanish-American War veterans. It is on the 4th Avenue side of the Square, in the middle of the block. Here, we see a drinking fountain placed inside a canopy shaped like a large clam shell. There is an inscription:

IN HONOR OF
COMPANY H 2ND OREGON VOLS
FOR SERVICE IN THE PHILIPPINES
MAY 15, 1898   AUGUST 7, 1899
DEDICATED TO THE CITY
BY THE
MOTHERS, SISTERS, AND WIVES
MDCCCCXIV

Company H was one of the companies composing the aforementioned Second Oregon Volunteer Regiment. The fountain was donated to the city by the "Ladies Auxiliary of Company H." At the time of the war, Company H was made up of young, unmarried men. Their mothers and sisters organized the auxiliary, which flourished actively long after the war. In later years, as the veterans married, their wives, too, became members of the auxiliary.

On January 23, 1914, the auxiliary announced it would donate a drinking fountain, which could cost up to $450. And there would be a prize of $50 to the winner of the design contest. The designs had to be submitted by February 16, giving the contestants just three weeks to prepare their entries. City Commissioner W. L. Brewster selected the site for the fountain.

An Advisory Committee was formed to make the selection. It included representatives of the auxiliary, two architects, and also C. E. S. Wood, who in 1885-86 had been instrumental in selecting the sculptor for Portland's Skidmore Fountain. This jury acted speedily. On February 18, just two days after the close of the contest, they announced the winner: John H. Beaver, an architectural draftsman. It is his design that we see today, though its stone decorations have been grievously eroded by sun and rain. For his $50, he was also required to supervise the construction of the memorial.

The fountain was dedicated at a ceremony on September 2, 1914. Charles E. McDonell, who had been Captain of Company H in the war, presided. Rev. Cullen E. Cline, a Methodist minister, gave the opening and closing prayers. A Boys' Drum Corps, composed of sons of the Company H veterans, assisted in the program.

As to the inscription, May 15, 1898 is the day when members of Company H were mustered in at Portland and left by troop train for San Francisco. August 7, 1899 is the day when they were mustered out of service at the

Presidio in San Francisco, having arrived back there on July 13th. And here again, the Roman numerals refer not to wartime events but the year of the dedication, in this case precisely.

Besides these evocative memorials, Lownsdale Square has other pleasing attractions—its magnificent trees of many species (elms, cedars, pines, ginkos, etc.) which alone make a visit, a leisurely stroll, worthwhile.

No Bars on the Bears

THERE ARE SEVERAL good reasons to visit our zoo. Well worth it, just for itself, is the zoo train. Pulled by a wistfully evocative steam locomotive, it will take you from the Rose Garden to the zoo. Once there, you can have a deli lunch and, as a divertissement, watch the monkeys scratching themselves indelicately and eating each others fleas. And, of course, you can see all the other animals of Noah's Ark. Also, you can admire the congenial design of the zoo as a whole. To create it required imagination and careful planning. Though there have been many changes in subsequent years, the zoo's ambiance still reflects the original vision of the architects who conceived it. The architectural work was done, during the years 1955-59, by the firm of Lawrence, Tucker, and Wallmann.

I visited their office occasionally while they were designing the zoo, and though that was many years ago, I remember (with the help of some notes and writings) our conversations. It will help you to enjoy and appreciate our present zoo to know how the architects created it.

Portland's old zoo, the one prior to 1959, had been so inadequate, with its mangy animals cramped into prison-like cells, that my first question was, "Will the animals be any better off in the new zoo?"

"Definitely," said Mr. Lawrence, and he explained that the architects had been working on the zoo plans for three years and had studied the designs of zoos all over the world. "The first thing we had to do was to get acquainted with the animals themselves." The architects concentrated on zoos in cities in the same latitude as Portland, whose problems of heat and ventilation are similar.

"What about those zoos where the animals have plenty of room to run around?" I asked. I was thinking of the far-ranging and panoramic Bronx Zoo. "Can't we have something like that?"

Their answer was twofold. First, the limitation of space. The area available was only about 40 acres, which would need to be intensively developed. There just wasn't room for the creation of an African veldt on which lions and giraffes could roam freely. Then there was the question of the object of the zoo. "Do you want people to *see* the animals?" as Mr. Lawrence put it. "In the Bronx Zoo, the animals are usually so far away that you can't see them. We are planning an *exhibit* zoo."

But, said the architects, that wouldn't mean animals in cages. Most of the animals would be in "grottos"—recessed areas, on eye level with the public and separated from them only by open moats. Behind the grottos would be chambers into which each species could retire. Every animal, however gregarious, occasionally tires of being stared at, and desires some privacy. The animals would be fed in those inner chambers, which would not be open to or visible to the public.

Mr. Tucker explained that the size of the moat would depend on the species. The moat around the tigers, who are great broad-jumpers, would need to be 25 feet wide. That is enough, according to experience at other zoos, to keep even the most agile tiger from being tempted to leap over it. The moat around the wolves would need to be only 16 feet. While tigers would have only a moat enclosing them, leopards and other climbing animals would have to be behind bars. The foxes would also be behind bars, so that viewers would be able to get closer to them than with a moat. "To see and smell foxes, you have to be close to them," the architect explained.

The bears, they said, will stare you right in the eye, just across the moat, with no bars to obscure the view.

In each of the grottos, the architects planned to place "fixtures" or "furniture"—objects to keep the grottos from being utterly barren. In a sense, each grotto was to be something like a "set" on a theatrical stage. The "sets" being designed by the architects were completely stylized. There was no attempt to create the illusion of natural setting by imitating trees or rocks in concrete. Instead, the animals would be living in a world of "architectural free form"—sweeping curves, geometrical and abstract shapes. It would be, I thought, like spending one's life confined in the sculpture court of the Museum of Modern Art. How that might affect an animal's psyche was hard to imagine. But, over the years, the tenants seem to have suffered no apparent neuroses.

There were, it was obvious from those conversations, many challenging architectural problems in planning a zoo, and Abbott Lawrence, Ernest Tucker, and George Wallmann came up with interesting innovations. In general, they visualized the zoo as a place to appeal to many sorts of people, both natives and tourists, and in that, we may now say, they succeeded handsomely. The architects defended vehemently their zoo-train concept, which they believed would be very popular, and a money-maker. That enthusiasm has been fully justified by its subsequent popularity.

Since that original design, the area available to the zoo has been increased from 40 to 64 acres. Now included is a four-acre African Area, which replicates the open bush country of East Africa. So the zoo is continually changing and evolving.

The Case of the
Missing Park Blocks

EVERY PORTLANDER has enjoyed, one way or another, the South Park Blocks, which extend from Jackson to Salmon Streets. Along those arbored, grassy, and statue-laden squares are the city's cultural oases: museums, theaters, some historic churches, a university. The North Park Blocks, too, extending from Ankeny to Glisan Streets, though less elegant and inviting, provide some welcome greenery. What a pity, people often say, that our city's founding fathers didn't set aside for parks that entire row of blocks, including those between Salmon and Ankeny Streets. We would now have a parkway all the way through the urban center.

Well, that was, in fact, their intention. What went wrong? It might be supposed—hearsay would have it so—that an original landowner's will was broken in order to turn what had been designated as public property into private ownership. Actually, the truth is rather the opposite—there was no will, only good intentions. It is a tangled tale, the conclusion of which seems to be that our loss of those park blocks was due to carelessness or ignorance of the law.

Five townsite pioneers owned this land when our story begins. Theirs are well-known Portland names. From south to north across the townsite they were Stephen Coffin, William Chapman, Daniel Lownsdale, Benjamin Stark, and John Couch. The five agreed, it appears, that there should be a strip of park blocks across the entire townsite. There are references to such an agreement, though the archives contain no formal document substantiating it. Perhaps it would be more accurate to call it "an understanding." In any case, the circumstantial evidence is plain. Early maps and plats of the townsite show the blocks not only between Jackson and Salmon but also between Salmon and Stark Streets as park blocks. Also, the six blocks between Salmon and Stark are half the size of other city blocks—that is, 100 feet wide—but exactly the same as the blocks that did become park blocks. And the streets along the entire strip were named Park and West Park.

Mr. Lownsdale was the principle advocate of the plan for the park blocks. He may have been inspired by the urban parks and parkways in the old cities of Europe, which he had visited in the 1840s before coming to Oregon. But the other claim owners went along with the idea. However, though the original city plats showed all the park blocks from Stark Street south to Jackson Street, no legal transfer to the city of the title to those South Park Blocks was recorded.

As for the North Park Blocks, John Couch carried out his part of the understanding. He received formal title (the "patent") to his claim in January 1865. (The wheels of the Federal Land Office did turn slowly—he had taken up that claim in 1845 and applied for it under the Donation Land Act in 1850.) On January 25, 1865, he donated to the city the land for the park blocks from Ankeny to Glisan Streets. They were shown in his plat for "Couch's Addition."

Between the North and South Park Blocks was Benjamin Stark's claim. It was a wedge-shaped parcel only the tip of which was in the line of the park blocks. Instead of platting that portion to provide two park blocks, he laid it out as two irregular polygons, which he sold as private property. His claim didn't fit neatly into the city's checkerboard pattern because of the acute angle at which his streets (Stark, Oak, and Pine) converged on Burnside Street, as shown on the accompanying map.

(Aside: The reason for this aberration is that Captain John Couch laid out his streets on True North, whereas the older Portland plat of 1845 was surveyed on Magnetic North, which deviates from True North by about 21 degrees. This creates some interesting angles where the two plats meet, along Burnside and Ankeny Streets.)

Mr. Stark was an absentee landowner. He lived in Portland intermittently in the 1850s but left in 1861 when he became Oregon's U.S. Senator. Thereafter, he lived in the East. Apparently, he had second thoughts about donating the two acres to the city for parks. He did offer to *sell* the land to the city, but at a price that was far above the current values in Portland. Possibly he based his "selling price" on land values in New York and Boston, which hardly applied to a frontier townsite. As a result, that land remained as private property and those two potential park blocks were lost.

The owner of the portion of the townsite between Salmon and Stark Streets, with its potential six park blocks, was Mr. Lownsdale. It was clearly his intention that they should be park blocks. But he neglected or postponed making a formal legal dedication that would transfer ownership of the six park blocks to the city.

Daniel Lownsdale (1803-1862).

At this point, we must immerse ourselves in the complexity of the Lownsdale marriages and heirs. In July 1850, Daniel Lownsdale married Nancy Gillihan. They had what our attorney friends like to call "lawful issue"— namely, two children, Ruth and Millard.

Nancy died April 15, 1854. The *Oregon Weekly Times* of April 22 published this item:

DIED

In this city [Portland] on the 15th inst., after a short but painful illness, NANCY, wife of D. H. Lownsdale, Esq., aged 33 years.

Mrs. L. was one of the old residents among us who was loved and respected. She was faithful to her friends; and Christian fortitude and resignation characterized her dying hours.... Her funeral took place at the Methodist Chapel on last Sabbath, the 16th.

Nancy died without having made a will. Her property, therefore, would go to her legal heirs—her husband and children.

On October 17, 1860, six years after Nancy's death, the Federal Land Office issued Daniel Lownsdale the "patent" (final formal title) to his claim. That patent designated the east half of the claim as belonging to Daniel and the west half to Nancy. The dividing line (line A-B on the accompanying map) was a few feet west of the street we today call Broadway. That is, the potential park blocks were in Nancy's half. Nevertheless, Daniel seems to have assumed that he and his children (of whom he was now legal guardian) had inherited all of Nancy's interest, so that he was now, in effect, sole owner of his entire Donation Land Claim.

Daniel Lownsdale died May 4, 1862, at the age of 59. His body was buried in Lone Fir Cemetery. He also had neglected to make a will. (Death does come at unexpected and inconvenient times.) So the property passed to his legal heirs. But who were they? Daniel was a widower when he married Nancy in 1850. By his first wife, he had

The "lost" park blocks in the Lownsdale Donation Land Claim
are numbered 1 through 6. The line A-B shows the division
between the halves of the DLC allocated by the Federal Land
Office to Daniel and Nancy. The heavy dotted lines show the
approximate boundaries of the DLCs.

also had lawful issue, to wit: James P. O. Lownsdale, Mary Lownsdale, and Ida Lownsdale. So there were five heirs of Daniel Lownsdale: James, Mary, Ida, Ruth, and Millard.

But there were other claimants. Unfortunately, or perhaps fortunately, Nancy, too, had been married before. She was a widow when she married Daniel. By her previous husband, Mr. Gillihan, she had two other lawful issue—Isabelle Gillihan and William Gillihan.

So there were seven children, who might be catalogued (from Daniel Lownsdale's point of view) as "mine, ours, and yours." And there was also an inheritance consisting of some of the most valuable real estate in Oregon. Hardly surprising, then, that the question of the division of the property came into court. It was an involved case which went on for more than a year and in which, I am afraid, avarice (sometimes called "my fair share") may have played a small role.

The complaint was filed April 27, 1864, and the case was tried in the Circuit Court of Judge Erasmus Shattuck. Basically, it was the Gillihans vs. the Lownsdales— the children of Nancy by her first marriage against Daniel's children. Were the Gillihans entitled to a portion of the inheritance? The fate of the park blocks was, therefore, only one aspect of the case.

Counsel for the Lownsdales attempted to show that Daniel had bought from Nancy, sometime between their marriage in 1850 and her death in 1854, all her interest in the claim. Unfortunately, they could produce no document supporting that assertion. And even if some informal arrangement had been made, nothing had been recorded, as a legal transfer of title, at the Court House. Therefore, the alleged purchase was not admissable.

From then on it was clear sailing for the Gillihans' lawyers. They asserted, successfully, that when Daniel Lownsdale made a plat of his claim, he didn't own the west half of it. He didn't have a title that would have enabled him to make a legal survey or to dedicate blocks for park purposes or for any other purposes.

By 1864, of course, all the streets were in place (having been surveyed and platted by Daniel Lownsdale) and many of the blocks in the west half had buildings on them. So the Gillihans announced that, "in consideration of the public good and convenience," they were willing to adopt and accept Daniel Lownsdale's map, "except for any dedication of any squares or blocks to the public." That is to say, No Park Blocks! All of the so-called park blocks in Nancy's half, they asserted, "are private property, and title to it is held by her heirs."

"Her heirs" included, of course, not only the Gillihan children but also her two children by Daniel Lownsdale. Therefore, the heirs most inconvenienced were the three children of Daniel by his first wife, and their descendants. But most of the property in both halves of the Lownsdale DLC had by then been sold to various and numerous other people. In all, more than 80 property owners were involved. By Judge Shattuck's rulings in 1865, they received or had to pay diverse sums of money in order to achieve an equitable distribution of the Lownsdale legacy. The significant bottom line, as far as our story goes, is that there would be no park blocks between Salmon and Stark Streets.

There remained the park blocks (numbered 7 to 20) from Salmon Street southward. Nothing had been built upon them and they were generally recognized as city property, though only on the basis of the 1852 plat map. As with the Lownsdale park blocks (numbered 1 through 6), no deed had been recorded to transfer their title to the city. In September 1870, the city agreed to pay William Chapman and his wife Margaret $6,500 for a clear title to the seven park blocks between Salmon and Mill Streets (numbered 7 through 13). Included in the transaction was

The park blocks at the intersection of Park Avenue and Montgomery Street, looking southwestward, in 1882.

the Chapmans' interest in the two Plaza Blocks bounded by S.W. 3rd, 4th, Salmon, and Madison Streets. There were some small adjustments, because the city check made out to the Chapmans, dated September 22, 1870, was for $6,250. That amount, for nine acres of urban property, must have been substantially less than the market value, so that the transaction was partially a gift.

The park blocks south of Mill Street, in Stephen Coffin's claim, were identified as city property in a plat filed December 7, 1867, but here again there was no clear title. On October 26, 1870, the city council voted to confer with Mr. Coffin, who had moved to Ohio, to find his terms for conveying the title to the city. The transaction was completed in July 1871. The city paid the Coffins $2,500 which, too, must have been partially a gift.

The city council and some of the townsfolk were still not reconciled to the loss of the Lownsdale park blocks. The council appointed a committee to find out from the owners of park blocks 1 through 6 what they would ask for them. The committee reported July 27, 1870, that the owners would sell them for $6,000 per block, but added, "Your committee, believing the price asked entirely too large, did not proceed further with the negotiation...."

On September 7, 1870, the council offered $3,000 per block for those six park blocks between Stark and Salmon Streets, to be paid in 10-year city bonds, bearing interest at 8 percent. The offer was refused.

A year later, that $6,000 asking price looked like a missed bargain. Real estate values had doubled, and continued to rise. In a last effort, the city council put together a tax levy that would have provided $92,000 for purchasing park blocks 1 through 6. An election was scheduled for December 20, 1871. But the proposal evoked a storm of opposition. After all, in the Portland of that day, the great outdoors was all around, and the fields and forests were only a few steps away. Way pay that enormous amount of money for six blocks of grass! To visualize the future benefits of a row of park blocks through a large city required imagination—a commodity which is sometimes in rather short supply. So the election was called off.

In subsequent years, there have been discussions from time to time as to how the city might acquire the six "lost" park blocks in the Lownsdale Donation Land Claim. In 1907, the voters approved a $1 million bond issue for parks, but that was used to buy Mt. Tabor Park. Later, a proposal for a $2 million bond issue for parks, which might have been used partly to buy park blocks, was voted down. Perhaps as a sign of defeat, the street that had been called "West Park" was eventually changed to "S.W. 9th."

However, we have since then recaptured one of those blocks for park purposes. In 1973, the block bounded by S.W. Park, 9th, Washington and Stark Streets became a park or plaza, "O'Bryant Square." It was bought by the city with the financial help of the Federal Department of Housing and Urban Development. It is now a scenic block with benches, trees, a fountain, and underground parking. It is named for Portland's first mayor, Hugh O'Bryant.

As of the summer of 1991, another of the "lost" park blocks, that between Yamhill and Taylor Streets, is vacant. All of the buildings have been demolished, and the rectangle is entirely naked. A thin layer of asphalt covers it and it is a parking lot. Perhaps such changes may offer the city the opportunity to recapture the other "lost" park blocks from time to time.

The tower of St. Mary's Academy (1890-1970).

Saints Mary and Patrick,
by Kleeman

TWELVE SISTERS from the convent of the Holy
Names of Jesus and Mary, in Montreal, set forth
September 16, 1859 on a journey to a "foreign mission."
Their assignment was to establish a school in Portland.

The trip must have been an adventure. From New York City, they sailed on the S.S. *Star of the West* to Panama. One visualizes them in their traditional black habits, walking in pairs around the ship's promenade deck in brisk constitutionals. They crossed the Isthmus in a railway car and boarded the S.S. *Golden Age*, bound for San Francisco. There, they changed to the S.S. *Northern* to come up to Oregon. When the ship dropped anchor, off Fort Vancouver, cannons were fired in a military welcome. It was a nice gesture, but the salute was not for the Sisters; it was for General Winfield Scott and his staff, who had been on the same ship.

The Sisters came to Oregon at the request of Archbishop Francis Blanchet, also from Quebec and formerly a parish priest in Montreal. He was appointed Vicar General of the Oregon Mission Field, and arrived at Fort Vancouver in November 1838. He was later made Archbishop of Oregon. He decided to establish a school in Portland, and in 1857 he purchased two city blocks from Daniel Lownsdale. They were bounded by 4th, 6th, Market, and Mill Streets. On this property Mr. Lownsdale had built a large, two-story house, which at the time was "in the midst of a forest at the edge of town." When the Sisters arrived, they moved into that house, which became their residence and also the school building.

The school, St. Mary's Academy, opened Monday, November 7, 1859. That was only 17 days after the Sisters reached Portland, which shows that they were efficient and determined. It was the first Catholic school in Portland. The first public school had been organized in 1856.

When the Academy opened, there were six pupils: three Catholics; two Jews; and one Protestant. They were all girls. The school was and has remained a girls-only institution. Music and art courses were in great demand, such cultural amenities being in short supply on the western frontier. A rectangular piano, which the Sisters with commendable foresight had ordered during their brief stay in New York City, arrived in February 1860, via Cape Horn. "The solitary instrument was seldom silent during the day," according to early accounts.

An additional building, the chapel, was built in 1863. In 1866, a massive stone retaining wall was constructed around the school grounds. This became necessary because of the grading of Fourth Avenue, which theretofore had been unimproved, and also because of the opening up of Mill Street, a development which the Academy had unsuccessfully opposed. For the wall, its builders used stone which had come as ballast in an English ship which was then loading in the Portland harbor.

A very tall Sequoia tree, gracefully conical, was a conspicuous feature of this block for nearly a century. It was planted in 1870—a slip was brought back by the Sister Superior from a visit to California.

By 1871, 250 girls were attending St. Mary's Academy. In those days, private schools were much more important, proportionally, than they are today. There were also 250 pupils at the "Portland Academy and Female Seminary" (a Methodist Church institution), 100 at St. Helens Hall (a girls school of the Episcopal Church), and 180 at Hebrew and German-language schools. And there were other smaller private schools. Altogether, in 1871, 860 students were attending private and church schools, and 915 were in public schools. Most of the students at the private schools were girls, while most of those at the public schools were boys. Did this partial segregation of the sexes help the students keep their minds on their studies? That is a debate which we must not enter into here!

The immediate success of St. Mary's Academy is surprising, perhaps, since only two of the original twelve

Sisters were English-speaking. The rest spoke French. The Sister Superior, writing to the Mother House in Montreal in 1864 to outline plans for expansion, pleaded, "Send us Sisters who are acquainted with this difficult language!"

The school was mentioned favorably by early writers. Joseph Gaston, in his *Portland, Its History and Builders*, praised St. Mary's, "from which have gone out thousands of Noble Young Women, taught, strengthened, and fortified for all the duties of Life by the self-sacrificing Sisters."

With the growth of population in the Northwest, the St. Mary's community established many other schools. One of them was in East Portland. It opened in 1886. The Sisters who taught there lived at St. Mary's Academy and commuted daily, on the Stark Street Ferry. In 1887, the first Morrison Street Bridge was built, which made the commute easier. In 1893, that school was taken over by the Catholic Diocese, which thereafter provided teaching staff. Among other schools founded by the Sisters was St. Mary's High School, at Medford, Oregon. It opened in 1865 and has been in continuous operation since then.

During all these years, the Lownsdale house continued to be the St. Mary's Academy school building, but it was becoming less and less adequate. The Sisters began to plan for a new, larger, and more worthy facility. In 1889, the old Lownsdale house was razed and construction began on a four-story structure with an elegant cupola and handsome facade. Architect for this building was Otto Kleeman.

Mr. Kleeman's architectural legacy was extensive and varied. It included large buildings, Victorian houses, apartments, churches, convents, and monasteries. He was the architect for the early buildings at Mt. Angel Abbey. His first drawings for that work were made in 1883. Unfortunately, those wooden buildings were later

St. Mary's Academy in 1890, shortly after its completion and dedication.

destroyed by fire. The only structure surviving from the Kleeman era is the small wooden chapel by the cemetery. Though he was awarded contracts for many Catholic churches and Catholic institutions, he was not himself a Catholic—a pleasingly ecumenical note.

Otto Kleemann (later simplified to Kleeman) was born in Germany March 13, 1855, and he received his degree in architecture there. He emigrated to America and went to San Francisco, where he worked as a draftsman for several architects, meanwhile learning English. In 1877, he married. He and his wife and children came to Portland in 1880. Here, he was employed as a draftsman by architect Justus Krumbein. His drawings, as initialed, must always have been "O.K." In 1882, he went into the architectural business on his own. He was 27 years old.

St. Patrick's Church in 1890, at about the time of its dedication. At its rear can be seen the temporary wooden building which served the parish until Otto Kleeman's classical structure could be completed.

When Mr. Kleeman began work on the new St. Mary's building, he was also doing the drawings for St. Patrick's church at N.W. 19th and Savier Street. St. Patrick's cornerstone was laid March 17 (St. Patrick's Day, of course), 1889. Both St. Patrick's and St. Mary's Academy were dedicated in 1890. They had some architectural similarities; both were variations of classical style with a dome or cupola.

St. Patrick's is often called "Portland's oldest church building." Actually, the Episcopal "Ascension Chapel" was slightly earlier. Its cornerstone was laid June 2, 1888 by Episcopal Bishop Benjamin Morris, who held the first service there in July 1889. But the building was later moved one block to its present location. Therefore, St.

Patrick's may properly be called the city's oldest church building in continuous use at its original location.

The city's northwest residential area was growing rapidly in the 1880s. Most of the original settlers in the neighborhood around 19th and Savier Streets were Irish immigrants. The Catholic Bishop decided to form a new parish there. The land was purchased from Dr. Rodney Glisan in 1887. A wooden building was put up in 1888 to serve parish needs until Mr. Kleeman's monumental edifice could be completed.

Otto Kleeman had many other interests besides architecture. For example, he was active in the German societies which flourished in Portland in the late nineteenth century. A letter he wrote gives an amusing insight into some of the goings-on among this segment of our population. In 1889, a German saloon, restaurant, and concert hall opened at what today would be 1040 S.W. Washington Street. It was called the Palmengarten ("Garden of Palms") and was named after a famous beer garden in Frankfurt, Germany. Otto Kleeman was the architect of Portland's Palmengarten, which had a saloon with billiard tables and behind that a large dining hall with a stage for musicians. The proprietor was another German immigrant, Otto Nussler.

The *Oregonian* in the past printed a column of historic curiosities called "Twenty-Five Years Ago." In that column, on February 25, 1914, was a paragraph about the opening of the Palmengarten a quarter of a century earlier. In response to that souvenir, Mr. Kleeman wrote this "Letter to the Editor," dated February 26, 1914:

Limburger in the Conerstone

The little item in "Twenty-five Years Ago"
of the building of the Palmengarten for Otto
Nussler brings to my mind a few incidents

which may prove of some interest to your older readers.

Going along the street to the contemplated cornerstone laying for the Palmengarten, I met Harvey Scott [editor of the *Oregonian*] and Jerry Caldwell [one of his reporters]. I told Mr. Scott where I was going and asked him to let Jerry come along to get a description of the ceremony. When Jerry arrived at the scene and found the "cornerstone" to be a tin tobacco box enclosed in four bricks and containing a piece of limburger cheese and a pretzel, he got wild. "Dash it," he said, "What did you get me into? The old man will want a good item, and I'll catch the devil."

Jerry stayed, however, and after witnessing the ceremony of mixing the mortar with beer, listening to all the German speeches, and assisting in disposing of a fine banquet, he did not care whether he ever got the item or not.

The building was for a number of years the meeting place of Germans and their families. There we would sit down, each family at its table, and have some luncheon and a glass of beer and listen to the music of the orchestra, or the singing of Joe Gschwander and his Tyrolean troupe. Joe was in his prime one of the world's finest zither players.

Mr. Kleeman was a good judge of that music because he was himself an accomplished musician and also an orchestra conductor. In the 1880s, he and some friends formed a "double quartet." They met at the Kleeman home every Sunday. The two quartets would play alternately; those not playing would listen and then criticize those who had been playing! In 1891, this grew into a 36-piece orchestra, called the "Haydn Symphony Orchestra." Otto Kleeman was its conductor. That orchestra was the precursor of the Portland Symphony Orchestra.

The details of all the other interests and activities of Mr. Kleeman would be distracting. We might just note that he was, for 17 years, Grand Adjutant General of the Indian War Veterans of the North Pacific Coast, an organization of old-timers who liked to reminisce at annual conventions called "encampments." He was a founder of the Lang Syne Society—clearly, he was a bit of a romantic! And he was an active member of the Masonic Lodge, having joined Willamette No. 2 Lodge in 1885.

All this time, he was busy with architectural work. During 1889-90, he designed the Mt. Tabor suburban railway. He was consulting architect for the old *Oregonian* building, at S.W. 6th and Alder Street, in 1892. In 1904, he was the architect for the Arminius Hotel, at 1038 S.W. Morrison Street. It was built by the German Aid Society, which still owns it, and was named for a German general (Arminius is Latin for Hermann) who defeated a Roman army in A.D. 9. The name of the building was later changed to the Morrison Hotel, and it is now a "historic architectural landmark." Two of the houses Mr. Kleeman designed have also been declared "historic architectural landmarks." They are at 2030 and 2036 S.W. Main Street.

Over the years, St. Mary's Academy flourished in the spacious building Otto Kleeman had designed. College courses were added. That department was transferred to a separate location, Marylhurst, in 1930. The high school department continued at St. Mary's Academy.

Unfortunately, it seemed that the Academy's 1890 building couldn't last forever. By the 1960s, maintenance was becoming a problem. And the building was inadequate for the growing student body and its needs. The

Sisters decided to build a new building. Across the street from the old St. Mary's Academy building was the other block bought by Archbishop Blanchet in 1857. It is bounded by 5th, 6th, Market, and Mill Streets. That block became the site of the new St. Mary's Academy building. Part of that building was completed by 1965. In 1967, the Sisters announced that the old building, which had been standing there since 1890, would be abandoned and sold. There was an outcry from sentimental Portlanders to whom that old building and its tower had become quintessential "Portland." And, indeed, it was inspiring, rising above surrounding structures and, as we remember it, a glorious sight, especially in moonlight. The ink drawing at the head of this article portrays that tower. But, as the Sister Superior said at the time, "We can't afford to keep that building as a historical landmark; we need all of the money for the new addition." She said that the building itself was of little value because of the high maintenance and restoration costs. The property was sold to a developer for $705,000, all of which represented land value.

The new building is a two-story brick rectangle, strictly functional. It does, of course, meet all the requirements of the municipal building code, though it had no architectural pretentions. There, nevertheless, the Academy and the Sisters continue their teaching tradition with distinction. The Academy has recently won several national awards for teaching excellence. We conclude that it is not so much the edifice but rather the Spirit that counts, a thought which we will grasp firmly as we think nostalgically of the old building.

In 1970, in a cloud of dust and debris, the building wreckers brought down Otto Kleeman's structure. It had served well for 80 years. Otto might well have been saddened. But, two miles to the northwest, his St. Patrick's Church stands solidly. In 1970, at about the same time his St. Mary's was coming down, St. Patrick's was declared a "historic architectural landmark." In 1974, it was placed on the National Register of Historic Buildings, all of which means that it cannot be altered in any significant way. It has recently been completely refurbished, and there seems to be no reason why it should not last "forever."

On the entablature over the columned entry, in large bold letters, is the phrase *"GLORIA IN EXCELSIS DEO."* So St. Patrick's will be proclaiming through the coming centuries "GLORY BE TO GOD ON HIGH"—with, perhaps, a little bit left over for Otto Kleeman.

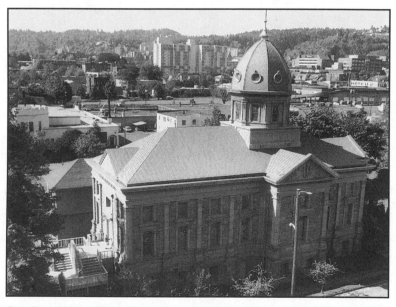

St. Patrick's Church in recent years. Note that the original classical pyramid of steps has been replaced by stairs with railings.

An 1885 Facade

PORTLAND WAS ONLY 34 years old in 1885 when Joseph Bayer, a manufacturer of metal cornices and decorations, built a two-story brick structure on Second Street between Madison and Jefferson Streets. He had come to Portland from San Francisco in 1879. In his new building, his shop and office were on the ground floor. On the second floor, he and his family lived—a sensible old-world arrangement whereby the daily commute to work was simply walking downstairs.

Mr. Bayer employed his art lavishly on the facade of his building. Carved medallions, no two of which were alike, were inserted among the bricks. An elaborate balcony, graced with griffins and fit for a King or Pope to appear upon, was placed atop metal scrollwork. The whole building was set back a few feet from the sidewalk, slightly recessed relative to the adjoining buildings. The total effect was pleasant and inviting.

That gracious and venerable building was torn down some time ago, but before that happened, I paid it a respectful visit. Its address, as a result of the renumbering of Portland streets in 1931-33, had become 1215 S.W. Second Avenue. Mr. Bayer's business was no longer there. Part of the building was being used by a sheet metal fabricator, but most if it was empty and dilapidated. Few passers-by seemed to notice the curious structure, even though it was an architectural period piece.

The medallions and decorations on the front of the building, which at first glance appeared to be stone, were pressed metal. The technique was often used in the 19th century for facades and cornices, and for ornamental ceilings in office buildings and homes. This was the process:

1. The design was made in soft plaster.

2. When the plaster had hardened, a mold was cast from it in type metal, an alloy which in its liquid molten state can reproduce the tiniest details but which is very hard when cold.

3. The mold was put into a press. The press would bear down heavily on a sheet of metal which thereby took the shape of the original plaster design. Mr. Bayer used a ten-ton press to make the ornaments for his building.

Examples of this sort of work can still be seen on surviving buildings in Portland's "Old Town" area. Some of them may well have been made by Mr. Bayer, although I can't substantiate that.

In the *City Directory* of 1887, Mr. Bayer had an informative full-page advertisement. Among other things, he dealt in "galvanized iron cornices, Bickelhoupt's patented metallic skylights, and terra cotta chimneys." He added, "Country orders promptly attended to."

Perhaps because of his enterprise and promptness, but also, no doubt, as a result of the rapid increase of population in the community, Mr. Bayer's business grew. In 1908, he moved to larger quarters just two blocks away. After inspecting the old building on Second Avenue, I walked over to the firm's newer location, where the business was being continued by his descendants. It was apparent at once that Mr. Bayer had decorated this building, too, and the ceiling of the office was an elaborate example of the metal-stamping art. The walls of the office were lined with dusty files of records going back to 1879. That building, too, has now been demolished, but at the time of my visit, the work was still going on there.

One of the employees was sitting at a typewriter, in a musty and windowless corner. We said to her, "People interested in architecture think it's too bad that old buildings like this are being torn down." She replied, "Some of us don't think they're being torn down fast enough."

Johan Poulsen's
Wooden Castle

DRIVING ALONG McLoughlin Boulevard or down the east end of the Ross Island Bridge, you may see, if you dare avert your eyes from the streams of traffic, a historic landmark, a century-old castle with a conical spire. A safer and more satisfying way to see it is to park on an adjacent street and walk.

The house is enormous. It has three stories, and the ceilings are 12 feet high. The pointed tower reaches up about 50 feet. There are winding staircases, several fireplaces, and nine bedrooms. There is a bedroom on the first floor for the maid—and surely there would be a need for some domestic help.

This mansion was built in 1891 by Johan Poulsen, a partner in the Inman-Poulsen Lumber Company. From his house on the bluff, Mr. Poulsen could look down on his lumber mill, located on the river bank below him. He also had a panoramic view of the river and the city center.

The sawmill and this castle were both part of a great building boom that was going on in Portland around 1890. The expansionist era had begun in 1883, when the first railroad was completed connecting Portland with the eastern states. Easier access brought in a flood of immigrants, and the rail link also improved the marketability of Oregon products. From 1883 to 1891, the population in Portland and vicinity doubled. That building boom led to a great demand for lumber. Two men who had come to Portland earlier and were already working in the lumber business saw the possibilities and formed a partnership to create what became one of the largest lumber mills (at one time, the largest) in the Pacific Northwest. Mr. Poulsen's partner was Robert D. Inman. Their Inman-Poulsen mill, at the foot of S.E. Clinton Street, had a wharf which would accommodate two ocean-going ships.

Both partners built wooden castles on the bluff overlooking their mill. The Inman house, on the corner of 6th and Woodward Street, was one block north of Mr. Poulsen's. It was almost identical to the Poulsen house, including the three-story tower. The Poulsen house (and probably the Inman house, too) was built of premium-quality wood. An inspection at the time of its designation as a historic landmark showed that Mr. Poulsen must have been on the lookout at his sawmill for extra-large structural beams and the best possible lumber.

The Inman house survived until 1958, when it was demolished to create a parking lot for the Dairy Cooperative Association plant. The ornate mansion, with gables, balconies, and spooky recesses, looked like a suitable setting for an Edgar Allan Poe mystery story. When it was pulled down, a photo of the collapse was published with the headline "The Fall of the House of Inman!"

The name of the architect for the Poulsen and Inman houses isn't known, and it's quite possible, even probable, that no local architect was involved. That was the time when there was widespread use of "plan books"—books which contained all the plans for assorted houses, even ornate ones like our wooden castles. Houses very much like Mr. Poulsen's can be seen in many mid-western cities, where they are cherished as historic relics of the 1880–1900 period. The style is sometimes called "American Queen Anne." It is likely that such plans were chosen by Mr. Poulsen and given to a local builder-contractor who would make whatever modifications the site or client required.

Johan Poulsen bought the land for his castle, a tract 100 x 100 feet in the "Villa Heights" plat, in July 1890 for $3,000. The house was completed about August 1891. He sold it August 3, 1891 to S. B. Willey. So the Poulsens lived in this house for only a very short time, a few months at the most. Why didn't Johan and his family stay in the magnificent castle? According to one account, Mr. Poulsen fell under some financial constraints and had to sell it. We do know that during the years from about 1891 to about 1895, there was a national economic squeeze, which hit Portland particularly hard. Boom is always followed by bust (just as nemesis always follows hubris), and the bigger the boom the bigger the bust. That depression reached its nadir in the "Panic of 1893." The Portland *City Directory* for 1895 notes that "the business stagnation which has hung so gloomily over our country for a few years is now passing away."

But Mr. Poulsen's financial embarrassment, if any, must have been brief, because by August 1892 he had built and was living in another house, almost as large and impressive. It was on the lot where the Red Lion Inn in the Lloyd Center now stands. The Poulsen family lived there on Hassalo Street for many years.

A different explanation for their sale of the castle on the bluff is mentioned in a family archive, namely, that

Mrs. Poulsen (Dora) didn't like the castle! That is, as we know, a wife's prerogative, for which no explanation is necessary. But we might guess that she found the chateau-like residence not quite "homey," and the work necessary to maintain it burdensome.

Title to the Poulsen house passed through many hands. Mr. Poulsen had sold it to Mr. Willey in 1891 on a mortgage. The title reverted to Mr. Poulsen on July 14, 1894, on which day he sold his interest in the property to Arthur Zwicker for $7,500. In 1902, it was bought by William J. Clemens, an insurance agent. In 1919, it was bought by A. A. Hoover. Mr. Hoover was in the bakery business and was called "The Doughnut King"—he was listed that way in the *City Directory*. So the house became known as "King's Castle!"

The sawmill and castles were only later episodes in what had already been a series of wanderings and adventures for each of the two partners. Johannes Poulsen was born in north Slesvig (at that time part of Denmark) in 1849. The area was annexed by Prussia in 1865 and, when the German states were united by Bismarck, it became part of Germany. Johannes, therefore, is sometimes called an immigrant from Germany. But in 1920, as a result of a plebiscite, north Slesvig was returned to Denmark. So it is probably more accurate to call our lumberman an immigrant from Denmark. In any case, he left his birthplace in 1870, at the age of 21, and came to America. He worked in the lumber business in Iowa. There, he married Dora in 1873. They came to Portland in 1875, and Johan (he had simplified Johannes) went to work for the Willamette Steam Sawmill Company, at the foot of N.W. Savier Street. By 1885, he was secretary-treasurer of the business and also of the North Pacific Lumber Co. In 1890, he sold all of those interests and pooled his capital with that of Robert Inman to form the Inman-Poulsen Lumber Co. It was incorporated in July

1890 with a capital of $75,000, and Mr. Poulsen was secretary-treasurer. He died in 1929. Johan and Dora had five daughters.

Robert D. Inman was born in Ohio in 1853. He was four years younger than partner Poulsen. Robert attended school when he could, but in those days boys were obliged to spend most of their time helping the family in the struggle for a living. Though he had little schooling, he didn't seem to miss it, as we shall see. He began his working career at the age of eight, as a tow-boy on an Ohio canal. In 1865, now 12 years old, he joined a wagon train of pioneers heading for Oregon. Here he worked on a farm from 1865 to 1869. He then came to Portland. He recalled in later years that when he arrived in Portland, he went up to Council Crest and looked down on the town. "Something in the sight stirred me. I sat down on the grass and kept looking a long time...I started out to make my fortune, with nothing but the clothes on my back, but I had no fear. There was not in my mind the suggestion of a doubt that I could make my own way."

He got a job cutting railroad ties, as $1.25 a day. Next, he became a brakeman and fireman on the Oregon & California Railroad. Then he worked for two years for a John Wilson Circus! Unfortunately, the record doesn't tell what he did for the circus. Could he have been a clown? Probably not; his character and various vocations seem to suggest a more mechanical job.

In 1875, he started to work at the Willamette Steam Sawmill Company, where he met Johan Poulsen. First, Robert piled lumber, at $2 a day. Then he became a machinist. Reminiscing about his early jobs, he said, "I was fascinated by mechanical appliances and every chance I got I studied how they were made. After two years, I was given charge of the planing department."

That same year, 1875, perhaps on the strength of a good job with a future, Robert married Frances Guild.

She was a daughter of pioneer settler Peter Guild. She was born in 1857 on her father's farm near "Guild's Lake" in N.W. Portland.

In 1882, Mr. Inman was one of the incorporators of the North Pacific Lumber Co., of which Mr. Poulsen later became part owner, too. In 1889, Mr. Inman sold all his other interests and in 1890 formed the partnership with Mr. Poulsen. Mr. Inman was president of Inman-Poulsen Co., which, by 1903, was the largest lumber business in Oregon, with 350 employees. Later, its employment reached a peak of 700.

In 1891, the Inmans moved to the east side, to be near the new mill. Until that time, their address had been "South Side, Guild Lake." In 1892, their home was on East Sherman Street. By 1893, they were residing at East 6th and Woodward Street, the address of their castle on the bluff above the sawmill.

Mr. Inman was active in the Democratic Party, and in 1892 he was elected to the legislature. In 1900, he was elected a state senator. He was also a Shriner and a member of a number of other Masonic orders. He and Frances had two daughters, Minnie and Idy. Frances died in 1909 and Robert died in 1920.

Inman-Poulsen Lumber Company was a large plant, extending over many acres. At the north end of the property, a great mound of sawdust accumulated continuously, deposited by a conveyor belt leading out from the sawing plant. Next to the sawdust mountain was a power plant of Portland Electric Power Company (predecessor of P.G.E. Co.). The power plant used the sawdust to make steam for generating electricity. It was a beautiful example of industrial symbiosis, where the waste of one industry becomes the input or food of another industry. It also had the less practical but more amusing aspect of providing a conversational topic for predicting future weather—so it was alleged. The size of the enormous sawdust mountain would vary, you see, with sales of lumber and need for electricity. Old timers claimed they were able to predict the severity of a coming winter by the height of the sawdust pile—winter's thermometer level to vary inversely with the height of the sawdust pile that autumn. The logic behind such a forecast has never been explained satisfactorily. I *do* see that the sawdust pile (call it the "SP Index") might be an ultra-sophisticated (and utterly fallacious) tool for forecasting the stock market.

A New Stall for an Old Steer

PORTLAND'S *GOLDEN STEER* is 100 years old this year, 1991. He hardly looks his age, though it is mature even for an animal carved out of wood. Indeed, he has never been in better form. Now in his latest and probably last stall—on display in the museum of the Oregon Historical Society, where he receives the constant care of curators—he looks like going on forever.

During most of his life, he stood patiently on the roof of the Perkins Hotel, which for 70 years graced the northeast corner of Washington Street at 5th Avenue. The hotel was built by and named for Richard S. Perkins, who made his money in meat and livestock. The *Golden Steer* was conceived, so to speak, by Mr. Perkins. It was a tribute to cattle and cattlemen. Mr. Perkins instructed the architect for his hotel, Justus Krumbein, to supply a statue of a steer, to be placed in a conspicuous place at the top of his hotel. Architect Krumbein gave him all he asked or could have wished: a stall framed by stone ornamentation and recessed into an enormous haute-baroque tower. The tower rose above the six-story hotel and dominated its facade. There, seven stories above the street, in a shrine befitting some medieval prince's monument, the architect placed a life-sized steer carved from cedar. The steer was painted with gilt and illuminated at night by the very latest gadgets—electric light bulbs! The hotel opened February 4, 1891, which, as we shall see, was Mr. Perkins' 68th birthday.

Mr. Perkins welcomed the patronage of his friends from eastern Oregon, eastern Washington, and Idaho, and cattlemen made his hotel their headquarters. They liked the *Golden Steer*. Also, the hotel had an excellent dining room, as noted in this announcement from 1894:

> The veteran Portland restaurateur, Mr. D. H. Simmons, whose skill as a caterer is appreciated by epicures, conducts the Perkins' restaurant. He numbers among his patrons many businessmen who have dined with him for years. Meals are served at all hours at the Perkins restaurant, for from 25 cents up.

During the 1890s, the Perkins Hotel was next in importance in the city after the chateau-like Portland Hotel, which had opened some months earlier, on April 7, 1890. But cattlemen stayed at the Perkins. The *Golden Steer* made them feel quite at home. And he was a conversation piece for everyone. He was almost like the statue of a saint in a shrine. Certainly, he was a graven image. But as far as we know, no one bowed down to him—at least not for the record. If we are to believe the stories of the day, his fame became international. It was said that sailors arriving in port would, as soon as they could get their feet on land, make haste to the city center, asking,

"Where is this here *Golden Steer* we've heard about?"
Such were his days of glory.

But a nation wide financial crunch—the Panic of
1893–94—brought trouble to Mr. Perkins, as to
thousands of others who had gone into debt to pay for real
estate ventures. His hotel had been an expensive project,
embodying first-class construction and up-to-date no-
tions—electricity, for example, and almost unheard-of
luxuries such as rooms (some of them) with their own
baths! Here is a description from the periodical *West
Shore*, December 20, 1890, when finishing touches were
being put on the hotel:

> The building is built of brick on a massive
> stone foundation.... It is 100 x 100 feet square
> and has 160 rooms, aside from the first floor,
> where are located the office, barroom, barber
> shop, restaurant.... Electricity will be used for
> lighting purposes, though gas has also been
> provided. The rooms are sumptuously fur-
> nished and Brussels carpets are used
> throughout. Light and ventilating wells are
> introduced in the center of the building in
> such a manner as to admit plenty of light and
> fresh air to all the rooms. Steam heat is
> provided for every room, and electric call bells
> connect all parts of the house with the office.

Though Mr. Perkins had substantial capital of his
own, the lavish expenditures on his hotel forced him to go
into debt. Then, in 1893–94, interest rates shot up, and it
became almost impossible to borrow money to pay off
loans. He struggled with his financial problems for two
years, but in 1896 his creditors took over the hotel. While
they were deciding what to do with it, they put in their
own manager, C. W. Knowles. Mr. Perkins and his family,

who had been living in the hotel, moved to a house on
N.W. 19th. But the *Golden Steer*, for the time being,
remained *in situ*.

In 1906, the owners sold the hotel to Lot Q. Swetland.
Mr. Swetland was not a cattleman. Our *Golden Steer*
suffered the indignity of being not wanted. He was
removed from his ornate shrine and locked in a dusty,
windowless attic room on the top floor of the hotel. He
languished in that limbo for 18 years.

In 1924, Arthur Everett Myers took over proprietor-
ship of the hotel. Mr. Myers was not a cattleman, either,
but he liked the steer. And the affluent ranchers from the
east had, for years, been inquiring about their mascot.
Mr. Myers' first official act, upon assuming command,
was to have the steer taken out of the attic, regilded, and
returned to his stall in the tower. He also changed the
name of the establishment to "The New Perkins Hotel."

The years passed. The *Golden Steer* remained in his
shrine, but he was neglected. The lights went out. Less
and less golden, but on the contrary, whitened by pigeon
droppings, our steer felt far from the range, far from any
deer or antelope, and he must have thought of many a
discouraging word. Also, his vista was becoming narrowly
circumscribed. When he was first tethered in his magnificent stall, in 1891, he could look down on the entire
town. The towers and steeples of churches were almost
the only structures on his level. By the 1940s, he was
fenced in by high buildings, and he could contemplate
only the traffic on the streets below. There he had seen,
over the decades, many changes—horse-drawn buggies,
then electric streetcars, and then automobiles, and more
automobiles, and more automobiles!

During all those years, numerous articles were writ-
ten about our *Golden Steer*. In one, he was called a calf!
Perhaps that author was influenced by childhood Sunday
School lessons about the Golden Calf, the one Aaron

madeth in Exodus. Other writers called him a cow. Sometimes he was called a bull. No! Those writers either couldn't get close enough to see the critter or else they knew nothing about bovine anatomy. The *Golden Steer* has horns, almost as long as those as a Texas longhorn, but not quite. Certainly, he has none of the other anatomical curiosities which would qualify him to be anything but what he is and always will be—a steer.

In 1956, the Perkins Hotel property was bought by a savings & loan association, which planned to tear down the gracious old building with its bay windows, and replace it with a flat-chested modern structure of colored glass and aluminum. In 1957, building inspectors declared the hotel a fire hazard. The cost of upgrading it, to meet building standards as a hotel, was considered by the new owners to be too high, since they planned to tear it down soon. So the upper floors were closed. But the stores along the street level remained open. One of them was Rich's Cigar Store, a Portland landmark for many years. High up in his tower, above the now empty hotel rooms, our steer remained in isolated neglect.

When demolition of the Perkins Hotel began, the *Golden Steer* was given to Lipman's store. He was placed in the basement in the "Men's Clothing" department— perhaps the store's nearest approximation to a cowboys' tack room. While his new location was a bit subterranean for a range animal, at least he was dusted regularly, and he received what must have been gratifying attention after years of neglect. Also, no more pigeon droppings.

When Lipman's was taken over by Fredrick & Nelson, in 1979, the *Golden Steer* was given to the Oregon Historical Society, where he will remain, his wanderings finally at an end.

The life of Richard S. Perkins was even more varied and peripatetic than that of his steer. He was born in Bristol, February 4, 1823, Bristol was a busy port in

The Golden Steer, *descending on ropes from his shrine on the roof, when the hotel was about to be demolished. He was on his way to become a conversation piece in a department store.*

western England, and as a youth he must have enjoyed the romantic setting, with sailing ships gliding down the Severn River estuary outward bound to distant countries, especially America. Remember that it was from Bristol that the *Hispaniola* sailed for *Treasure Island* with Jim Hawkins and Long John Silver aboard. That memorable event took place, according to R. L. Stevenson, in "17—." It was a few years before the time of Richard Perkins, but the scene was much the same.

Richard himself came by sailing ship to America in 1851, when he was 28 years old. That year, he got as far as Ohio. In April 1852 he started for Oregon. To pay for his food and transportation, he drove four yoke of oxen across the plains. He reached Portland late in November 1852. Here, he went into partnership with Arthur Harrison Johnson, to operate a meat business. Mr. Johnson was also an Englishman, having been born in London in 1830. "Johnson & Perkins" had their slaughterhouse near what is now N.W. 23rd Avenue and Flanders Street. Their retail meat market was in the center of town.

In April 1857, Mr. Perkins, then 34 years old, married Elizabeth East. The ceremony took place in Polk County, at the home of the bride's father.

About 1863, Mr. Perkins left the meat partnership and went into the cattle-droving business. One might have thought that those seven months driving oxen across the plains had been enough for a lifetime, but Mr. Perkins evidently enjoyed it. He liked the gentle herbivorous quadrupeds, he liked the wide open spaces, and he was comfortable in the saddle. During the years after 1863, for some of his ventures, he bought herds of cattle in the Willamette Valley and drove them to Idaho. On one occasion, he started out from Oregon with 4,000 sheep, to shepherd them to California. Before he reached his destination, he had an opportunity to sell them at a nice profit. With the money, he went to Texas, bought 4,000 cattle and herded them to Oregon.

These activities took Mr. Perkins away from home for weeks at a time. What Elizabeth thought of all this is not recorded. Apparently, she accepted it good-naturedly, and everyone was happy. They had ten children.

With the energetic outdoor life he loved, and the strenuous business of herding cattle, one would have pictured Mr. Perkins as a formidable figure of a man. But descriptions (more impressionistic than statistical, it must be noted) say he was small and slight, but with piercing blue eyes. Whatever else, he was a bundle of energy. That eventually begins to ebb, however, and when he wanted a somewhat less exhausting life, he stopped cattle-droving and started a large ranch in Washington County, where he engaged in farming and stock raising. He had 5,000 cattle and 500 horses. Even that got to be a bit much, and in 1886, at the age of 63, he sold his ranch and, with the money, took over a hotel in Portland, the Holton House. It was located on the corner of 4th and Alder Street. He conducted that hotel for four years. During that time, he and his family lived in the Holton. Two of his sons, Richard A. and John A., were clerks in the hotel. In 1890, he contracted for the construction of his Perkins Hotel. He had owned that 100 x 100-foot parcel of land for several years. When his new hotel opened, in February 1891, he and his family moved there. Another son, Robert S., joined the staff, as porter and driver of the hotel's carriage, which met passengers at the railroad station.

The house on N.W. 19th, to which the family moved in 1896 after the financial difficulties to which we have already alluded, was Mr. Perkins' home for the rest of his life. There, in April 1902, after a long illness, he died. He was survived by Elizabeth and all ten of his offspring— eleven if we count the *Golden Steer*.

The Old Morrison Bridge (1905—1958), with its draw open. Note the operator's cabin in the center of the open draw span.

One Long and Three Shorts

THE FIRST BRIDGE across the Willamette River at Portland was the Morrison Bridge put up in 1887. It was a toll bridge, which meant that the Stark Street Ferry was able to compete with it for a time. That bridge was built of wood, though it had an iron draw, and its construction was such that you were required to hold your horse to a walk when crossing it. It was replaced in 1905 by what most of us remember as the "old" Morrison Bridge. This second bridge was completed just in time for the Lewis and Clark Centennial Exposition, and it was one of the wonders shown off to the visitors. It continued in use until May 24, 1958, when the present Morrison Bridge opened. If you lived in Portland before 1958, you remember the old bridge. It had a revolving or "swing" draw, which pivoted on a pier in the center of the channel. You may recall, from high school days, walking across that old bridge and, if you saw a riverboat about to require the draw to open, timing your walk so as to be on the draw when it swung around to open. What fun!

The draw was operated by a tender, who sat in a hut located in the middle of the draw. There, perched in his vibrating little gazebo above the roadway, he waited patiently for the occasional riverboat. I had often been curious about the tender's job, and even a little envious of his long periods of solitary leisure surrounded by the ever-changing panorama of the harbor. On a cold January day, shortly before the old bridge closed forever, I climbed up to that little octagonal hut and spent an instructive hour learning some of the details of the tender's trade.

Benjamin Popham was on duty. He was figuring his income tax. Only one person could sit down at a time in the tender's hut, and Mr. Popham motioned me towards the chair, a 19th century black leather armchair suitable for a judge. "I sit all day. Glad to have a chance to stand," said Mr. Popham.

"I've been an operator here since 1943," he told me, in answer to a question. "Came over from Burnside." He was referring to the Burnside Bridge, where he had worked previously. The tenders speak of the different bridges as though they were different countries, alien but not hostile.

Inside the hut were the various personal and professional paraphernalia associated with bridge tendering, including a pair of field glasses and a long-handled dipper for drinking out of a water bucket. "No running water, you see! We had to move the water bucket inside to keep it from freezing," said Mr. Popham. The temperature outside was a crisp 20 degrees (Fahrenheit, that is) and the river was mottled with broken ice. "First time in my experience there's been this much ice," he added, looking up the river.

"You must have a lot of time to read," I said.

"Oh, yes, we do some reading. We subscribe to some magazines." He picked up a copy of the *Saturday Evening Post*. "And the library brings us books once a month." Mr.

Popham indicated a wooden box in one corner, containing half a dozen books. "You can request books you want. The majority like Westerns. Some read mysteries."

"What do you read?"

"Westerns," he said with a shrug. "Just something to relax."

At one side of the hut, I saw what looked like the controls from an old streetcar. That, it turned out, is exactly what they were. The draw was turned by two streetcar motors, and 600-volt streetcar controls were used to operate them. The controls, of cast iron, were covered with the scrolls one associates with the nineteenth century. They bore the legend "Pat. Aug. 1883."

"When there were streetcars running on this bridge, we used to take the power for the draw right off the trolley wires," said Mr. Popham.

Far up the river, we could see a large tug and barge coming downstream. "May be the *Peter W.* They said it was up today. If they want us to open, they'll call. Our call is one long and three shorts."

We watched as the tug shoved its barge through the broken ice. Then the tug whistled—one long and three shorts. Mr. Popham took hold of a cord with an old-fashioned "Turk's head" knot on its end and answered with one long and three short notes from the bridge's shrill air whistle. The gatemen came out of their houses along the roadway, pulling on their gloves.

While awaiting this infrequent activity, the gatemen sat in little cabins attached to the sides of the bridge. In them there was running water and even a washroom, which the draw operator could also use. The job of the gatemen was to close the gates which prevented inattentive motorists from driving off the ends of the bridge when the draw was open. Draw service has to be maintained around the clock, and five operators and about a dozen gatemen were assigned to the Morrison Bridge alone.

"When I think I ought to open, I ring the bell," Mr. Popham said. It was a bell like the ones on old steam locomotives. "Technically, I should open as soon as the boat whistles. Sometimes I fudge a little, to let more automobiles get across. That's my responsibility."

When Mr. Popham had rung the bell and the gates had been closed against road traffic, he "pulled the wedges." They projected from each end of the draw and were forced by electric motors into slots in the stationary portions of the bridge. They held the draw in place and supported its ends.

"Well, here goes," said Mr. Popham, and he turned the handle of the streetcar control. Slowly, we began to revolve. "We can open the draw in only one direction now, because of those pilings for the new bridge."

While the tug was passing through, Mr. Popham made an entry in the log. Actually, it wasn't the *Peter W.* as he had first thought when he saw the tug far up the river. The entry read: "*Patricia* and barge. 3:42 pm. Coming down."

"The draw is slow. You have to judge. There's a lot of weight moving. It worried me at first. Oh, such a terrific amount of weight to get moving."

When the draw was closed and automobile traffic was proceeding again, I asked Mr. Popham if he had ever had any difficulties with the draw.

"This old bridge has a better record for working without breakdowns or repairs than any other bridge on the river. It's old but reliable. Only thing that stops it is high water. That shorts out our electrical connections."

"Once the draw got stuck when it was open. Power failed. I had a tugboat hitch onto the end of the draw and pull it closed. It was a question of tying up either river traffic or road traffic. Tied up river traffic for a few hours while it was being fixed. Doesn't take much to turn this draw, if you put a rope out on the end; it's so long, you have a lot of leverage."

"In the old days, when it got real hot, the draw used to stick. The steel would expand and the draw would just lock right in place. They came down several times and cut off an inch or so. Sometimes when the draw would stick like that, we used to call the fireboat—you can see it just there by the end of the bridge. They would come over and spray water on the bridge. The cold water was supposed to contract the steel, but it never worked very well. Then they put in an expansion joint and that cured the problem."

The old Morrison Bridge was Portland's lowest over the Willamette River, so it had the busiest draw. Tugs which could pass under the other bridges often had to whistle for the Morrison Bridge. During a typical winter month, its draw opened about 120 times—four times a day, on average. By contrast, the Burnside Bridge, as Mr. Popham recalled from his earlier work there, opens only three or four times a month in winter. But in high-water months, like June, all bridges' draws are busier. During the previous June, for example, the Morrison Bridge had opened about 750 times during that one month.

"We have to open for anything that whistles," said Mr. Popham. "We're over a navigable stream, as defined, and anybody can call, just a sailboat with a horn."

Bridge tenders also have other duties, as part of their job. They take temperature readings for the Weather Bureau and keep a record of the height of the river.

When the new Morrison Bridge opened, this venerable old draw closed forever. But at the time of my visit, the fixtures in the operator's hut were about as they had been in 1905, when the bridge was built.

I asked Mr. Popham about the new bridge. "Its draw will be wider, and higher above the water. And it will line up better with the Burnside Bridge—that will make things easier for the riverboat pilots. But for us here and now, the main trouble with this one is that the electric heat in this little cabin is either 'on' or 'off.' I sure hope they have thermostats in the next one!"

I came away from that pleasant interview much better informed about bridge tendering, but a little less envious.

The Rats around Us

ONE RAT for every human being! That's the estimate of the rat population in most cities today. They're here, but you probably won't see them. They try to keep out of sight. They're elusive because they've learned, over the years, not to trust *homo sapiens*, with whom they are obliged to share the territory.

Portland's rat population, however, may be a little less that 437,319—the number of people living within the city limits according to the 1990 census. That's because the city officials, in 1944, started a rat control program, after cases of bubonic plague had been found in Tacoma and some other West Coast port cities. Those were the war years, when there was a teeming traffic in transpacific shipping and when urgency sometimes superseded careful use of such precautions as rat-guards on the ships' moorings. There were no cases of plague in Portland; the control program was precautionary.

In 1944, funds were allocated for the City Health Bureau to employ a full-time rat expert. The city didn't provide major rat-extermination service. "Pest Control" remained, as it is today, a private enterprise. The city's role, rat-wise, was to inspect, to advise, to perform autopsies on dead rats, and to make tests of any fleas the rats may have harbored. (A bite from an infected flea is what gives people the plague.) The city did do minor de-ratting when citizens called for help.

Some time ago, we accompanied the city's Pied Piper on his rounds. Our first call was at an old house that was being torn down. An effort was made to check every building for which a wrecking permit had been issued. When rats find that their old home has been destroyed, they will, of course, migrate to new quarters.

We looked particularly for burrows around the base of the old house. If a hole two or three inches in diameter is found, with its edges smooth and polished, it's likely to be an active rat hole. This would be the Brown Sewer Rat, the species most abundant in the city. Two other species are also found here: the Black Rat and the Roof Rat. These latter two have tails and ears that are longer, in proportion to the body, than those of the Brown Rat. The Black Rat and the Roof Rat live in the upper portions of buildings. We found no evidence of rats.

The next call was at a new house whose owners had telephoned the Health Bureau. There was a neat hole by the foundation, close to an opening which gave access to the basement. It was in the basement that the family of rats were finding their food supply. The Pied Piper put, in the burrow entry, a few spoonfuls of crushed oats that had been soaked in powdered eggs and poison. It did seem like a rather mean trick, but we were unable to suggest a practical alternative.

It's something of an art to find the right poison for a rat. If rats are enjoying regular meals by their own foraging, their normal food may be more attractive than the poisoned bait, and they may ignore it. But often, their diet is deficient in fat. Then, some fatty food, loaded with poison, may attract them. Rats living around meat or rendering plants, however, get plenty of fat; there, you have to lure them with starches. And at some times of year, when rats are having difficulty getting enough water, they will take liquid bait.

The problem is something like that facing the subtle but vacillating fly-fisherman, as he tries to decide which fly to use to tempt "the wary trout." A "Royal Coachman" fly may work wonders on the Metolius River but be ignored contemptuously by the fish in the McKenzie!

For years, both the city and county maintained health programs and laboratories which duplicated each other to some extent. In the interest of efficiency and economy, the city discontinued its anti-rat and other health programs, and all such functions were assumed by the county. There is a contract whereby the city pays a share of the costs, but the work is now done by county employees. The department that is concerned with rats is called "Vector Control." A "vector" is a carrier, in this case, a carrier of disease. Rats, that is to say, come within the horizon of government officials only as disease carriers.

So far, we've been looking at the rat problem rather self-centeredly from our own human point of view. But our rats also have their problems. Their big problem is food. That's because rat population can grow very rapidly. Rats are tremendously fecund: they breed at the age of six weeks, and the females have litters every three months. Each litter numbers about ten. At an exponential growth rate of that magnitude, it would not be long before the entire surface of the globe would be carpeted with a continuous layer of soft, furry rats! That hasn't happened, of course, because there isn't enough food. Rats migrate readily in search of better food supplies. Also, they will eat almost any thing if driven to it: grease from machinery, colored crayons, even their young, which they

may regard as an unusual delicacy. Rats often get considerable help from people who feed birds—unless the birds' dish is something like a metal tray, with a rim, and suspended by a thin wire.

If a rat were informed of Mr. Malthus's *Essay on Population*, he would certainly endorse that gentleman's doctrine fully. Mr. Malthus, you may remember, was an English economist who, in the early years of the nineteenth century, became famous by pointing out (what had long been obvious to rats) that populations grow, unless their growth is restrained artificially, up to the limit imposed by the food supply. At that point, population is held in equilibrium with the food supply by famine, disease, and war—and perhaps infanticide. You won't find a rat who will disagree with that. Famine he knows. Disease may come about from crowding and malnutrition. And war? Rats have to fight with other rats for *lebensraum*. The infanticide we have already explained.

When Mr. Malthus was writing, birth control on a species-wide scale was not practical. The only restraint he contemplated was sexual abstinence, and, perhaps wisely, he did not put much faith in that. To what extent your rat would be willing to forego one animal pleasure (sex) in order to enjoy more fully another animal pleasure in the future (adequate and even gourmet meals), we are not sure. Abstinence may be a lot to expect from rats. They seem to be wired-up in such a way that the pleasure of the moment makes them say, "Let the future take care of itself!" Would birth control, if explained to them by some family planner, resolve this dilemma? Would they see it as a way for them to have their cake and eat it, too—so to speak? Difficult to know! On the rare occasions when we meet rats, they seem to be in too big a hurry to think about it—too busy trying to find something to eat!

Meanwhile, there is one rat for each one of us. We hesitate to offer our advice to them, since they are doing so well. They are adaptable and clever—quick at solving mazes, you know. They have conquered the globe. There is practically no place on earth to which they have not spread. If the measure of success is ubiquitousness, they are successful. In this respect, they are the peers of the sparrow, the startling, the housefly, and us humans.

Shrunken Heads
and a Wordy Bird

WHEN I ARRIVED at the Shoreline Trader, a second-hand store which for many years embellished a corner at West Burnside and Second Avenue, there was a sign in the door: "Back at 3:30." I looked at my watch. It was, by chance, just 3:28. Displayed in the store's window were dusty odds and ends, a diverse assortment of curious objects. My eye was caught by a used funeral urn, and I was trying to imagine the antecedents of the second-hand, or better, second-body item when, exactly at 3:30, the door was unlocked from the inside.

As I entered, I was startled by the twang of an out-of-tune zither. A metal finger projecting upward from the top of the door had scraped across the strings of the unharmonious instrument, which was mounted upside down over the entrance. Sets of gongs tied to the door were also activated.

Seeing my surprise, Ralph Sowers, the genial and slyly humorous proprietor of this Skid Row trading post, explained the reason for these precautions: "I like to know when someone comes in."

"You must have come in the back door," I said.

"There isn't any back door. I was asleep. I sleep in the back. I have a couch there. I take a *siesta* every afternoon. I set my alarm clock, though," he added, explaining his punctuality. "I cook a little there, too." Mr. Sowers, I found out later, is 64 years old.

When I told Mr. Sowers I just wanted to look around, he appraised me, silently, up and down, and finally said, "Sure, make yourself at home." After a pause, he muttered, "But keep your hands in your pockets."

Two shrunken heads, exercising a ghoulish fascination, were on a shelf. I had heard that Mr. Sowers had the shrunken heads of a man and his wife and that he wouldn't sell one without the other. I said that this was an example of business ethics of a very high order. "I like the story," replied Mr. Sowers, "but I can't say they were man and wife. I'll sell you either one...for the right price."

"You have to be very careful about your shrunken heads these days," Mr. Sowers continued. "There are a lot of monkey heads on the market. They aren't shrunken at all—they just start out small. Here's how you tell a real shrunken head." He picked one up, turned it over and pointed to some stitches up the back. "The skin's cut up the back and peeled off the skull and shrunken and then sewn together. Sometimes the fakes aren't even monkeys—just little pieces of leather that's been molded. Those are easy to spot." Mr. Sowers pointed to the eyebrows with a pencil. "On a real head, the eyebrows lie down. With fake ones, the hairs stick straight out— they've been sewn in."

It looked to me as if the eyebrows on the one he was holding stuck straight out, but before I could investigate

more closely, Mr. Sowers put it back on the shelf. "I really don't want to sell them," he said. "They bring in business. If somebody asks about buying them, I say the big one's $300 and the little one's $200. That usually puts an end to it."

The Shoreline Trader is full of conversation pieces, but the two most interesting ones are Mr. Sowers himself and a black myna bird. The bird's name is Joe, and he is very talkative. He is also politically conscious. His favorite remark is "I like Ike." Joe has a rich, clear voice. What sounds like a slight accent may be due to the fact that his parents came from southeastern Asia. But he himself was born in New York City, so his speech habits may contain remnants of Bronx dialect.

"Where are you from?" Mr. Sowers asked Joe.

"I like Ike," replied Joe.

"I know that," nodded Mr. Sowers, "but where are you from?"

"I am a Republican," answered Joe."

"I know that, too," said Mr. Sowers, with what seemed an almost saint-like patience, "but where are you from?"

Turning to me, he added, "I refused $150 for him yesterday."

I wondered what would happen if someone repeated that probably fictitious offer today, but I was not about to try the experiment myself, especially for a bird with such a one-track mind. But later on, when Joe warmed up to it, he revealed more of his vocabulary, which Mr. Sowers says includes about 60 words.

Joe lives in a rather roomy cage. He doesn't get to fly around much. "His droppings are too liquid," explained Mr. Sowers, waving a hand to indicate the varied contents of his store, "and you know what seagulls do to rocks."

"Before I got Joe, I had a parakeet. It was a fine bird...knew a lot of words...a nice, clean vocabulary. Then a sailor came in. He was around town for several weeks, and he used to drop by. He spent a lot of time talking to the parakeet. When he got through with that bird, I had to get rid of it."

"You mean you can't erase anything from a bird's vocabulary?"

"No, sir. Once he's learned it, he never forgets. If I catch anybody trying to teach obscenities to Joe, I make the..." Mr. Sowers caught himself just in time. Lowering his voice, he continued, "... I make the b-a-s-t-a-r-d leave."

"You don't think Joe can spell?"

"He's a smart bird but he doesn't care much for spelling," said Mr. Sowers, at which point Joe cawed disdainfully, "You are a Democrat!"

Mr. Sowers uses a tape recorder to teach Joe new words. It relieves one of having to spend long hours with the bird, repeating the same phrase over and over. Joe spends a lot of time in the tedious company of the tape recorder. A less wordy bird might find it boring.

The zither alarm sounded and a man and woman entered the store. They browsed around. "I may get that table," said the man.

"I am a Republican," said Joe, loudly and quite clearly.

The startled customer stopped in his tracks and looked around with a puzzled expression. Nothing more was said, so he continued, though in a somewhat watchful manner: "I could turn that table into a coffee table."

On hearing that, Mr. Sowers frowned, walked over to the customer, and said, "I wouldn't want that table made into a coffee table." He shook his head as he contemplated the desecration. "No, that table is not for sale." After a pause, he added, "But if you come in early some morning when I haven't made a sale yet, it might be."

Mr. Sowers runs his store very much as it might have been handled by W. C. Fields if the great comedian had ever made a two-reeler called "The Antique Shop." Indeed, the Shoreline Trader is more of a hobby for Mr. Sowers that it is a job. He owns the entire block in which the store is situated. Also in his block are other stores and two hotels, one of which he leases out. The other he runs himself..."a flop house," as he described it. "Mostly pensioners. One's been living there ten years."

"What does Mrs. Sowers think of all this?"

"She doesn't really approve. That's a picture of Mrs. Sowers when she was a baby." He pointed to a tinted life-size baby photo, hanging near an Eskimo kayak suspended on wires from the ceiling. I was afraid to ask him if his wife's baby picture was for sale.

Wandering through the accumulation of oddments in the Shoreline Trader— surely as bizarre as the contents of Dickens' "Old Curiosity Shop"—one might imagine it had been going for a century at least. The enterprise dates back only to the 1940s, however. At that time, Mr. Sowers had a little business of buying goods damaged in fires and retailing them here at this location. Then people started bringing in second-hand goods to sell. At first, he didn't buy them. But during the last few years, the business has taken on more of the character of an antique shop. "Antiques are just third-hand second-hand goods," explained Mr. Sowers.

Mr. Sowers says that his transactions are diverse. As an illustration, he recalled that, one day last week, a man brought in some clothes to sell. "I don't deal in clothes," Mr. Sowers told him. "But I've got something here I think you'd like to have," the man persisted. Out of a shopping bag, he produced a silk opera hat, snapping it open with nonchalant finesse as though he wore one every day. He then pulled out a dress coat with tails. Mr. Sowers was interested, but he restrained his enthusiasm and simply said, "I wouldn't buy them even if you had the pants, too."

"Ten dollars?" asked the man.

"No, I can't use them."

"Finally," Mr. Sowers said to me, "I got them for $4. The next day I saw in the paper where a top hat and tail coat had been stolen. So I called up the party and told him I had them. He's coming down to get them."

"I hope he pays you the $4 you put out for them," I said.

"Oh, he probably will," replied Mr. Sowers.

"He ought to be glad you're such a good bargainer. It might have cost him ten instead of four."

With what sounded like a laugh, Joe said, "I like Ike!"

(Mr. Sowers and his friend Joe are deceased now, and the site of his dealings in third-hand curiosities is at present the office of a weekly newspaper.)

The End of the Line

LIGHT RAIL, as it is now called, has come back. "MAX" is running to Gresham and another line is being planned to Beaverton. This is not, of course, a new concept. For decades, Portland had streetcars and interurban trolleys. Besides the historic interurban lines on the West Side, there was an extensive light rail system on the East Side. From a downtown waiting room at S.W. Second and Alder Street, the line crossed the Hawthorne Bridge, ran along the east bank of the river to Sellwood, and then branched into lines running to Oregon City and Gresham. But because of public preference for private automobiles, patronage had dwindled. By 1957, there was just one light rail passenger line still in service—the suburban trolley line to "Bellrose Station," at S.E. 136th Avenue near Foster Road. It was operated by the Portland Traction Co., a private utility which also ran the city's buses. PTCo was getting out of the unprofitable passenger service, and the Bellrose line was soon abandoned, too. But I remember a farewell ride on it, and my recollection will complement today's revival of Light Rail. It was one of the last trips the Bellrose line made, in February 1957.

It cost twenty cents to ride out to Bellrose. The trip took half an hour each way, and it was far more entertaining than most reels of celluloid. By that time, the "downtown" terminal had been moved to the East Side, because of the removal of rail tracks from the Hawthorne Bridge. The line started at S.E. First and Hawthorne. There, an old bus lay at anchor, for use as a waiting room. It gave a transitory air to the operation; one had the impression, which indeed proved to be correct, that PTCo could fold its tents and go out of the passenger business overnight.

One of the delightful things about the trolley was that the conductor and passengers were like one big, happy family. "Thanks for coming along," said the conductor to a customer who got off as the trolley pulled up beside the mobile waiting room. "See you this evening," replied the patron.

The relaxing, rhythmic click-clack as the trolley rolled along made us regret the passing of the railed vehicle. The line paralleled the river and offered some beautiful views of the city skyline. And it was fast—just eight minutes to Garthwick, at the southern edge of Sellwood.

The few passengers, as they got off at the succeeding suburban stations, had the pleasant habit of saying "Thanks," to which the conductor might reply, "You bet." One passenger who failed to sound the buzzer in time overshot his station by a couple of blocks. The conductor obligingly threw the trolley into reverse and backed up, to deliver the passenger to his station.

Another custom, dying but still preserved in the 19th-century life-style surrounding the suburban trolley, was for children to wave to the conductor, who benevolently returned the greetings. The trolley played at least a passive role in the lives of everyone living along the tracks (even if they didn't ride it) because at everyone of the innumerable road crossings, the conductor had to shriek four blasts on the trolley's eerie air whistle.

The conductor was surprised when we stayed on to the end of the line, having obviously come along simply for the ride. But that had happened before. "Are you a rail fan?" he asked. Sentimental souls, with atavistic tastes in transportation, made up a sizeable percentage of trolley patrons.

We could hardly expect PTCo to operate trolleys just for rail fans. But one had the impression that the company had shown little enterprise in sustaining its unprofitable passenger service. As one conductor put it, "They want to stop running them." Perhaps a common self-interest explained the camaraderie among conductors and patrons.

The conductors we talked to seemed to have more imagination than those who manage the company—but the latter must, admittedly, keep an eye on the bottom line of the profit-and-loss statement. One conductor said that if large parking lots were built at several stations along the line (and there is plenty of suitable land), people would leave their cars there for the day and ride into town on the trolley. Another thought it would speed up service a great deal if the level road crossings could be replaced by viaducts. "Drivers don't have any respect for streetcars anymore," he said.

"We lost some business when they tore down the waiting room at S.W. Alder Street," said a conductor. "Then we lost some more when we were cut off from the West Side and riders had to take a shuttle bus to downtown. But it held up pretty well. What really knocked the business off was when they stopped taking transfers on the city buses. You can't expect people to pay 20 cents to get into town and then another 20 cents just to get across the river."

When we got to the end of the line, three little urchins, who had been waiting expectantly, popped into the car and helped the conductor reverse the seats for the ride back. The conductor paid each of them a nickel, and they ran into a nearby grocery and soon emerged with popsicles.

At the end of the line, while he was waiting to start the return trip, the conductor telephoned the dispatcher's office. "They like to know when [and if?] we arrive," he explained. "Any news?" he asked over the phone. We had an impression of being at a very distant outpost. On the way back, a wild-looking pony raced playfully with the trolley for several blocks, a laughing expression on its unbridled lips. A red-mittened little girl waved joyfully was we passed.

Sources and Acknowledgments

The contents of this (as any other) "potpourri" are diverse and wide-ranging, and the sources of the information are equally so. Much of the material came from personal interviews. Among general sources for Portland history, the most helpful were the archives of the Oregon Historical Society Library. Its vertical files of newspaper clippings, scrapbooks, biography and pioneer files and indexes contain rich historical ore. Also, the Public Library's "newspaper index" had many useful references. The City of Portland's archives provided official records about the gifts of memorials to the city. The library of the Portland Art Museum helped with biographical material about the sculptors whose works are described in this book. Title and trust companies were able to provide records of land ownership for the stories about the Poulsen Castle and the Park Blocks.

Three less well-known sources can be mentioned specifically:

The Church of Saint Patrick, 1889-1989, published by St. Patrick's Church, Portland, Oregon, 97209.

Oregon in the Philippines, by C. U. Gantenbein, printed by the Oregon State Adjutant General, 1903. This contained useful information for the article "A Stroll Through Lownsdale Square."

The Sculpture of Berthold Schiwetz, a catalogue published on the occasion of a retrospective exhibition of his work in 1971, by the Birmingham Gallery, Birmingham, Michigan. This provided some biographical details for the article "Saint with Sandals and Birds."

* * *

Sources of the Photographs

St. Francis (pages 25-27 and 29), Joy on Council Crest (page 35), Joan of Arc (page 97), George Washington (page 104), and the photo of the author on the back cover were taken by Joe Heidel.

St. Patrick's Church (pages 140 and 145) are from the archives of St. Patrick's Church.

The following 14 photos are from the Oregon Historical Society, with the OHS negative number listed after the title:

David Thompson - CN017805 (page 2), Coming of the White Man - 25674 (page 13), David Campbell - 10689 (page 39), *Iris* - 13470 (page 64), Harvey Scott - 4391 (page 77), Battleship *Oregon* - 76905 (page 87), Henry Coe - 001264 (page 99), Statue of Theodore Roosevelt - CN019920 (page 102), Veterans' Statue - 20064 (page 110), Daniel Lownsdale - 13420 (page 126), Park Blocks - 734 (page 131), St. Mary's - 5602 (page 139), Steer on Ropes - CN006079 (page 164), and Morrison Bridge - 86466 (page 167).

The other photos are from private collections.

Index

7/13
917.9549
SNYDER